Mind Over Matter:
The Power of Emotional Intelligence

Mind Over Matter:
The Power of Emotional Intelligence

By

Ann J. Polya, Ph.D.

To order additional copies of this book, contact:
Xlibris Corporation
1-888-795-4274
www.Xlibris.com
Orders@Xlibris.com
117665

Cover picture by kind permission of Dr. Petia Prime.
It is entitled the "Angel of the Waves".

In memory of my parents, Paul and Barbara Polya; my friend Donald Bock; and my Schnauzer Winston Mai-Laur.

Acknowledgements

With thanks to my friends – Elsie Bickford, JoAnn H. Bock, Kathy Burke, Susan Dahlberg, Susie Klein, Gary Loffler, Noel Miner, Bob Plunkett, Kathy Petrillo, Petia Prime, Doug Ramsey, and David, Faith, Marie-Pierre, Max, Michael, Rosie, Sophie, Zoe of the Polya clan, for your contributions and bright ideas as well as their support and encouragement; also for the distractions provided by young Harley.

In particular, I want to thank Dr. Petia Prime for allowing me to use the painting on the cover of this book; it is called the "Angel of the Waves" that connotes a calming of the emotions of our turbulent inner world, thus allowing us to take charge of our lives. Dr Prime's website is www.E21C.org, where you can learn more of her teachings and works.

I would also especially like to thank JoAnn H. Bock for her superb work as copy editor and script adviser.

About the author
Ann J. Polya, Ph.D.

Ann J. Polya, Ph.D. is a certified Emotional Intelligence consultant and a certified ICF Executive and Personal Coach. She has several Master's degrees and a Doctorate in Behavioral Sciences. In her previous book on Brain Fitness she shows how to can attain and keep our minds sharp, and this book expands on the importance of emotions in our lives and how we can empower ourselves by boosting our Emotional Intelligence.

Her varied background spans three continents where she worked as a senior government official at the European Union, as a senior corporate executive for Pfizer both in New York and Europe, and more recently as a psychotherapist, consultant and coach, author and speaker. Originally from the UK she lives in Florida and Connecticut. She is currently training for her first sprint triathlon. She can be contacted at PowerofEQ@aol.com.

Also by Ann J. Polya, Ph.D.

Brain Fitness: Breakthrough Training For Those Who Mind

Synopsis

Brain fitness improves the way our Brains function so the processing is faster, more accurate and efficient; additionally it increases our memory power, improves our focus and quality of our lives. For Brain Fitness we need to ensure that we grow new brain cells that are dependent on a chemical reaction-induced by certain exercises, and we also need to ensure that the change is positive to benefit from vast advantages. We can do this at any age, and this book shows us how we can achieve Brain Fitness and give ourselves and others a wonderful gift.

Table of Contents

Preface

In my previous book, "Brain Fitness: Breakthrough Training for Those Who Mind", I wrote about how Brain Fitness improves the way our Brains function so that the processing is faster, more accurate and efficient; additionally how it increases our memory power, improves our focus and quality of our lives. It discussed how we can promote the cellular growth in the brain, and that positive change could lead to Brain Fitness, but that we have to guard against the change being negative or negated by the laziness of our brains to revert to the previous default setting. The good news is that we are not condemned to repeat ineffective and unhealthy responses all our lives.

We know that the Neuroplasticity of the brain, if correctly stimulated, allows us to learn new ways to interact. This promotes sharper minds. We can protect against our brain's tendency to revert to the "default" setting by following the valuable conditions outlined in the book; furthermore, we can powerfully reinforce positive Brain Fitness, plus developed Emotional Intelligence has its own innumerable valuable benefits.

"Mind over Matter: the Power of Emotional Intelligence" expands on the nature of Emotional Intelligence. This includes the ability to be self-aware of our own emotions, to be conscious of the emotions of others and to manage our emotions in all our relationships. This takes a focused approach and can provide profound deepening of our personal understanding and self-development. When we face little stress, we generally enjoy our relationships and what we are doing; but when conflict and stress emerge, we often move to protect our emotional well-being in ways we learned earlier in our lives. Some of those reactions serve us well, but as adults they may no longer do so; indeed they may now interfere with our achieving effective and satisfying relationships.

This book helps the reader make a targeted effort to develop our Emotional Intelligence, which helps expand our ability to enjoy a wide range of relationships. As human beings we all have emotions; they are an integral part of who we are. Denial or sublimation will not allow us to escape from this simple fact. By expanding our core Emotional Intelligence, we can better build our access to our feelings, better direct our emotions, thoughts, and desires, so that we are not prisoners of their power. Emotional Intelligence helps us curtail negative feelings and thinking and attain more balanced –yet flexible- lives that accord with our values.

The purpose of this book is to build Emotional Intelligence fitness to complement Brain Fitness so that we dramatically increase the probability of staying mentally and physically fit throughout our lives, improve our memory, empathy, self-knowledge, awareness of another, clarity of vision, better communication and leadership skills and improved relationships with an informed choice of relationship strategies.

In this way, we can partake of this wonderful and empowering gift that adds so much value to our lives. It allows us to act in ways that matter even if no-one is looking, because this defines us, and enables us to reclaim our soul.

Chapter One: Age Proof your Mind

"There are no victims -only volunteers"
Dr. Petia Prime

Our brains are responsible for most of the things we care about—language, imagination, logic, empathy, creativity and how we make ethical decisions. They define who we are, and differentiate each of us from each other. While we do need other organs to keep alive, it is our brain that is vital to our very essence. Moreover, we now know that our brain cells can keep growing throughout our lives and the resultant cellular growth can construct positive benefits of better memories and faster and improved functioning provided we ensure positive inputs into the brain circuitry; this positivity depends on our Emotional Intelligence. Consequently by ensuring appropriately developed Emotional Intelligence, we can benefit both from the advantage of brain fitness and also we will have sharper minds with more emotional balance and vastly improve the quality of our lives.

If, on the other hand, we allow that cellular growth to be less than positive- by strong negative emotions, we can stop the whole process of acquiring brain fitness and sharper minds. We are emotional beings and if, for instance, we love someone and it is neither reciprocated nor are we treated well that love will be replaced by another emotion, such as anger, that will dominate our thinking and behavior, and effectively snuff out our development towards brain fitness.

We can get a better handle on our emotions to blunt this effect by improving our Emotional Intelligence which empowers us to get a better knowledge of ourselves, of others and how we interact with other to the best effect; this helps us get a new perspective on our purpose and way of life and paves the way to boost our Emotional Intelligence and awareness so that we can reclaim our way in the world.

So acquiring Brain Fitness and sharper minds with all its benefit is the preliminary step with its inherent benefits and is complimented by boosting our Emotional Intelligence, which is necessitated by the fact that our brains are inherently lazy and, even with encouragement via repetition, will revert to default or the old way of doing things. Our major defense here is Emotional Intelligence that can counteract the Brain's inherent laziness by ensuring positive cellular growth giving the benefits of sharper minds- plus the benefits from developed Emotional Intelligence.

About Emotional Intelligence

Emotional Intelligence will help us prevent the brain from reverting to default and thereby depriving us the benefits of Brain Fitness. To have developed Emotional Intelligence means we are aware of our emotions, our own and those of others; this means an ability to be aware of, name and manage our own emotions while being able to be aware of, name, understand and relate to the emotion of others'. Additionally, we relate to others effectively, both at work and personally, drawing from our wide range of emotions so that we can successfully manage ourselves in relationships and apply adroitly the appropriate relationship strategy.

Emotional Intelligence will give us many additional tools that will enable a different perspective on our thoughts and emotional patterns and allow us to behave in a continuing balanced way. They help us boost our self-knowledge, manage our reactions, enhance our empathy and understanding for others and help us develop more effective relationships so that we are not at the mercy of powerful emotions and our consequent thinking causes us less pain.

With good self knowledge and personal self management we can get a better handle on our nature and preferences and how to learn ways to leverage our strengths. Better understanding of other people enables smoother relationships and more socialization. Furthermore, with developed emotional intelligence, as demonstrated by research by Daniel Goleman (1995, 2002), Richard Boyatkis, Annie McKee (2002, 2005) and innumerable others, show a correlation between Emotional Intelligence and being self-adjusted, finding it easy to connect with others, as well as being flexible, resilient, tolerant, optimistic and having effective relationships in addition to being more successful at all they do.

Brain Fitness

In this chapter we will look at Brain Fitness as this is the preliminary step towards having sharper minds; this is best complemented by

Emotional Intelligence, which can empower us to ensure the changes are positive and prevent the brain from reverting to the default mode that deprives us of the benefits of Brain Fitness and sharper minds, so that we have more emotional balance into our lives.

We can achieve Brain Fitness, with faster, more accurate and efficient brain functioning, and improved memory power, focus and decision-making by inducing activation of certain chemicals in the brain; this is supported by ample evidence, including my book on "Brain Fitness: Breakthrough Training for those Who Mind" (2009), that our brain cells keep growing throughout our lives. The resultant cellular growth can construct positive benefits or negative benefits.

Cellular Growth for Change

Science has demonstrated that we can induce change by stimulating the production of certain chemicals in our brain circuitry. This growth can be positive or negative. We always think of growth as positive but this is not always true. The brain can revert to the previous mode if the new message is not reinforced, or even worse if our emotions are crossed we can develop a stronger emotion with negative consequences such as fear or anger, or, for instance, we may develop tinnitus where the brain provides a sound –a dull ringing in the ears –instead of absolute deafness.

Our brains thrive on the ability to make such functional changes otherwise we would not be able to memorize a new fact or master a new skill, form a new memory or adjust to a new environment; nor would we be able to recover from brain injuries or overcome cognitive disabilities.

Our brains are pliable, elastic and changeable throughout our lives-irrespective of our age or genetics: indeed any adult brain is not like a hardwired machine but can expand and change and be re-programmed so that it is able to adapt to circumstances and environments.

Stimulation of the Brain

We can stimulate the brain and induce changes, although the changes need reinforcement via Emotional Intelligence and repetition to last.

To trigger the brain stimulation we need a number of exercises as well as a few conditions.

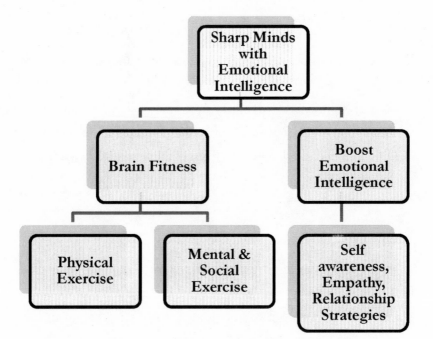

Image 1:- Positive Brain and Emotional Fitness

Exercises to Induce Brain Fitness

From the bottom left of the above diagram we can see that we need three types of exercises. These are Physical activities that account for 60% of the stimulation, and Mental and Social activities which together account for the other 40%.

Physical Activities

By far the largest component of ways to stimulate the path to Brain Fitness is by the use of Physical Exercise. It accounts for 60% of the chemical induction.

This can be working out at the gym on the aerobic machines such as treadmill or elliptical machines, walking and especially walking in nature, biking, bowling, and yoga or balance exercises.

We need to spend at least 30 minutes five times a week doing this form of exercise. Each activity has to be challenging to the brain so it represents new and untried ways of doing things. Thus, we need to push ourselves out of our comfort zone by increasing weights, difficulty or length of time so that we rise to confront the challenge.

Mental Activities

Contrary to popular myth mental activities, such as crossword puzzles only account – for approximately a quarter of the stimulation to our brains that promotes brain growth. These mental activities include mental posers, crossword or Sudoku puzzles, painting, playing an instrument, learning or speaking another language, or exploring different strategies in bridge or chess.

Our brains are learning machines and to keep them strong we must continually extend our repertoire by discovering and mastering new things that needs us to focus. This means putting in incremental effort that may stretch our abilities, use our listening skills that allow us to focus.

Social Activities

Socialization can involve meeting with a few others or even organizing meetings or any group activity. A substantial body of research suggests that beefing up our social calendar decreases your chances of memory loss and sharpens our minds. When we encourage others to work out with us or engage in mental exercise we are more likely to follow through and ensure that we are getting adequate challenge and novelty. The essential components involve intellectual and social activities that pose a challenge and different and yet are within our reach. This accounts for approximately 15% of the chemical induction.

As we expand our socialization skills we may find that we choose groups to match our views; in the words of Albert Einstein:

> *"Few people are capable of expressing with equanimity opinions which differ from the prejudices of their social environment. Most people are even incapable of forming such opinions."*

Social activity not only makes physical and mental activity more enjoyable, it can reduce stress levels, which helps maintain healthy connections among brain cells

Conditions to Maintain Changes

Emotional Intelligence

As we will explore in the next chapters, Emotional Intelligence is a vital element to ensure that the changes are positive and are in line with what we want, and consequently will dramatically allow the brain to revise the old default mode.

Additional Conditions to Promote Brain Fitness

Repetition

We need to repeat the path or mental track several times before the change sticks –even for a while. Our brains are innately laziness and will accept a different route when encouraged to do so by repetition, otherwise they revert to the "default" setting. This is why diets and giving up smoking or drink only work if the new command is sent to the brain repetitively, and this new mode in reinforced by Emotional Intelligence developments.

Novelty, Challenge and Focus

Each of the three activities, physical, mental and social must contain novelty, challenge and boost our need to focus.

Novelty

Where this is absent we will tend to operate in our comfort zones, and act and react in familiar ways as if we are acting on autopilot;

this may save energy but is boring and doesn't do anything to promote brain sharpness.

New experiences and events prompt our brain's machinery to switch gears in order to better master the new conditions.

Challenges

Life is full of challenges. We face so much data that we need to sift through to make sense, and we have to coordinate our reactions and juggle items so we move out of an automatic reaction or out of our comfort zone so that we push ourselves to achieve more. The most helpful for this purpose is when they are introduced progressively and we can achieve each by pushing out of our comfort zone.

Focus/Attention

In addition to novelty and challenge we cannot have change unless we pay attention and focus on what we are doing. Strong emotions such as stress often distract our attention and have a negative impact on brain cell growth. So we need to focus which can involve being selective, ignoring distractions and listening carefully.

How Can Brain Fitness Help?

With positive brain Fitness, as complimented by Emotional Intelligence, we can boost the performance in each of these are five core areas of our brains, which are:

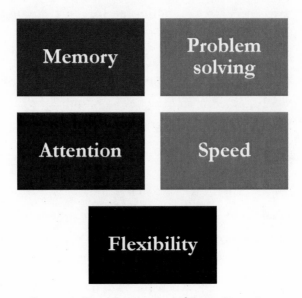

Image 2: Five Core Areas of Brain Function

i. **Memory**

We can exercise and improve our memories. Some examples can include remembering names after first introduction; recalling accurately an event someone was just talking about; recalling where you put something in the house; learning new subject quickly and accurately ; remembering names of plays you have seen and calculating figures in your head. This is accentuated with more developed Emotional Intelligence as that helps our emotional control, empathy, self-knowledge and relationship choices that all sharpen our minds so we can improve our memories.

ii. **Attention**

We know from studies that attention training can have a significant impact on our ability to perform well in sports and in tests as it increases our ability to filter out distractions and subsequently increases our productivity.

Some examples involve concentrating on a new challenge; driving safely and effectively; accuracy in sports like tennis or golf; peripheral vision and heightened focus on important tasks. With improved thinking we focus more clearly which improves our attention.

iii. **Speed**

Exercising our mental processing speed can help us think more clearly and quickly, improve reaction time, and increase alertness and awareness. We see solutions more easily and this helps us become sharper at work, school and throughout our lives. Some examples include accelerating our reaction time, being able to make decisions in time-sensitive situations, boosting our sense of direction and being able to adapt to new or different environments and building our capacity to visualize.

As we improve our speed of thinking and thinking things through, we can positively influence our thoughts and emotions.

iv. **Flexibility**

Switch things up with flexible thinking that is adept at adapting to different emotions. This enables multitasking to be a breeze, helps us articulate our thoughts better, and gives greater discipline to resist temptation. Getting better at flexibility can help improve our precision, cognitive control, and even your creative thinking.

Areas using flexibility skills include, strategic planning, multitasking quickly and efficiently, thinking outside the box, communicating clearly and being able to shift our focus of attention. We do not need all of these skills but we can pick the one we most want to improve.

v. **Problem Solving**

Need solutions? No problem. Better problem solving skills can help us make quick, accurate decisions. It helps make mental estimates, comparisons, and calculations, more easily and more efficient thinking and feel more balanced.

Some examples of this diverse category of cognitive skills and abilities include, recognizing patterns and trends, making quick estimations, comparing different values, and dissecting complex arguments.

"Use It or Lose It"

With brain fitness we need to use each of the component parts or we will lose that ability. Hence, if we do not keep using data—such as words, languages, names, we will no longer trigger reactions in the brain circuitry and the circuitry diminishes and eventually we cannot recall that word.

We can choose to activate chemicals to induce Brain Fitness and promotes our chances of possible success with repetition, novelty, challenge and focus to improve our memories, refine our mental acuity and agility, boost our problem-solving abilities; moreover if we develop our Emotional Intelligence we can make sure the changes are positive and happen- and not just revert to the old comfort zone. Plus, we can also increasing our self knowledge ability, heighten our empathy for others, and refine our relationship effectiveness.

The following chapters deal with Emotional Intelligence development which will help us revise the brains' "default" and pave the way for us to regain our purpose and our souls.

Brain Quiz No. 1

❖ Billy has 10 more marbles than Bobby

❖ Bobby has 6 fewer than Buzz

❖ Buzz has 15 more than Brenda

❖ Person with the least marbles has 20 marbles

❖ How many do all four have?

Chapter Two: Premier Minds Enabled by Emotional Intelligence

"Emotions …are at the root of everything we do, the unquenchable origin of every act more complicated than a reflex… In all cases, emotions are humanity's motivator and its omnipresent guide."
Thomas Lewis

It is in our brains that we store all the feelings and emotions we have ever experienced throughout our lives; it is where we also store all our thinking "software" needed to process and analyze new and memories. Our brains allow us to think, feel and act, make decisions, feel emotions and empathy and devise our purpose and meaning in live. Clearly there is every advantage to keeping them fit, and it is never too early to start promoting Brain Fitness.

Promoting Positive Brain Growth with Emotional Intelligence

We do want to ensure that the cellular growth does produce positive changes so that we can truly gain the whole package of advantages; the risk though is that as mentioned earlier, our brains are lazy and will want to revert to the previous mode unless we dutifully follow the brain fitness guidelines. Not only can we ensure the changes stick by expanding and developing our Emotional Intelligence, but we also benefit from the advantages of developing our Emotional Intelligence so that we gain greater control over our thoughts and emotions and improve our relationships.

What is Emotional Intelligence?

People with well developed Emotional Intelligence find relationships easy, enjoyable, and rewarding; are connected to others and are flexible, resilient, and tolerant of differences, are optimistic, trusting, good listeners and know their own moods and are observant of those of others and have emotional empathy while respecting boundaries.

While those with lesser developed Emotional Intelligence find relationships less satisfying, more easily disconnect from others or stay in unhealthy relationships for too long, are highly reactive, have a low capacity for chaos, tend to be rigid or brittle under stress, and can become immobilized, moody, resistant, or erratic, are less trusting of others and self, have lower emotional empathy for self or another, are tilted towards more action rather than feelings and miss some techniques to take care of oneself.

It is rare to find someone with perfectly formed Emotional Intelligence; indeed most of us have some areas to develop and this way we can find out what they are and in the process we will boost our self-understanding and personal growth.

The Expression "Emotional Intelligence"

The term Emotional Intelligence gained popularity in the mid-nineties with a book of the same name by Dr. Daniel Goleman. He stated that traditional IQ only accounted for a very minor proportion of success at work, while it was more successfully correlated to our emotional intelligence levels. Moreover he underscored that IQ levels remain stable throughout life, whereas emotional intelligence can be learned as can having a sharper mind. Indeed these two are interrelated and affect just about everything we do.

Despite the value we often put on our thoughts and reason, it is our emotions that are more powerful than our intellect. This point is emphasized in Reuven Bar-On's Handbook on Emotional Intelligence and the work of Daniel Goleman, Richard Boyatzis, and Annie McKee who state in their in their (2002) book on "Primal Leadership" that "…in moments of emergency, our emotional centers actually commandeer the rest of the brain, so leaders who are not emotionally intelligent…who can't keep check of their emotional impulses and correctly read the emotional temperature of a given situation—will simply not be effective".

Our Emotional Intelligence Profile

We all have our Emotional Intelligence profile that consists of our rankings in the dimensions of being self-aware of our own emotions, to be conscious of the emotions of others and to manage our emotions in all our relationships by quantifying our preferences for each relationship strategy. To obtain precise data we can do a test online by contacting an Emotional Intelligence consultant, such as this author, which simulates stress conditions so all the responses are those when we feel some pressure.

The resultant data measures our aptitude to access a wide range of emotions, our outlook-whether it is more optimistic or negative, our perspective on whether we look inwards to ourselves or outwards to others, our balance between what we feel, what we think and what we do, and our levels of empathy-both in terms of how well we assess another and how much feeling we have for what another is going through.

Moreover, the data calculates the kind of relationship strategies we use and our gives a ranking on how often we use them compared with the general Emotional Intelligence sample of the population.

By learning more about our own profile we can learn more about ourselves and where we may need some self-development; we also learn about how we react when under stress to protect our emotional well-being in ways we learned earlier in our lives. Some of those reactions serve us well, but as adults they may no longer do so; indeed they may now interfere with our achieving effective and satisfying relationships.

As human beings, we all have emotions; they are an integral part of who we are and there is no getting away from this simple fact. Emotional Intelligence takes this into account and sets up a means to help us ensure that our emotions do not monopolize our reactions; indeed the aim is to expand our core Emotional Intelligence, so that we have a wider panoply of emotions at our disposal, as well as our thoughts and actions, so that we are not prisoners of their power.

The following indicates the components of the Emotional Intelligence profile.

Emotional Intelligence deals with the range of feelings one can experience, whether one looks inward at oneself or outwards at others, a balance between action and thoughts and feelings,

EMOTIONAL INTELLIGENCE PROFILE

Access to Feelings

Empathy - Compassion

Positive/ Negative outlook

FOUR RELATIONSHIP STRATEGIES

Empathy accuracy

Self/ Other Outlook

Balance Feelings/ Thoughts & Wants

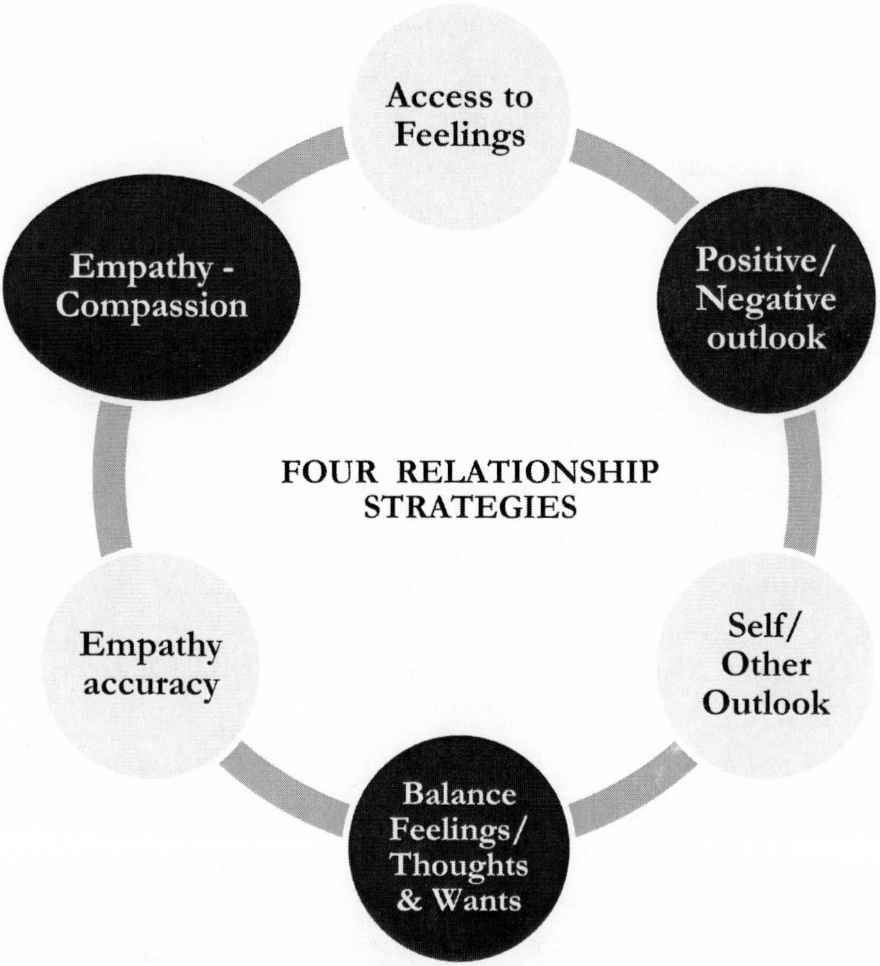

Image 3:- EQ Profile

and empathy—both characterizing the moment and feeling empathetic compassion and all of these elements match up with the type of relationships we tend to prefer—be they interdependent, independent, dependent or more disassociated.

We can measure our internal experience yielding a client profile of the dimensions of Emotional Intelligence by using a simple set of techniques that start by self reported reactions to video clips; the client watches the videos and also experiences some form of dissonance amongst the choices then this heightens the importance of the relationship and yield more enduring patterns. This data is computer analyzed and made available to client who discusses it in detail with a qualified Emotional Intelligence counselor. For more information to follow-up- please contact the author.

In Emotional Intelligence there are six dimensions and four types of relationship strategies that are impacted and impact the dimensions. Both the dimension and relationship strategies are interrelated and an impact of one set will affect the other set. They are represented by the following chart where there are two-way arrows between the dimensions and the relationship strategies.

Studies indicate that Emotionally Intelligent individuals are more likely to:

- Know and observe themselves better;
- Know their values and self-worth;
- Know their boundaries and maintain good connections even in the face of conflict or stress;
- Identify what is happening and be more tolerant and flexible;

- Have deeper appreciation of others and their motivations;
- Communicate better and be a good listener;
- Demonstrate empathy and compassion;
- Manage our own emotions and self-soothing;
- Adapt to different relationship strategies where appropriate.

Best Age for Emotional Intelligence and Brain Fitness

We can keep our minds sharp at any age and the earlier we start the better and it is helpful at all ages. It helps during the emotionally turbulent times of adolescence and young adulthood when we can go from elation to depths of depression over a phone call or lack of one, and equally so for our middle years or older having greater mastery over our thoughts and emotions is advantageous. As long as we feel emotions this will benefit us enormously. It helps us handle all hurly-burly of emotions and also the complacency that we often fall into as we mature since the big danger is that we feel we have life experiences and consequently do not have to pay so much attention. This is a fallacy. We always need to focus and pay attention otherwise we deter brain growth. This requires no special preparation, and it can benefit us all at any age from adolescence onwards through our middle and later years.

Adolescents

Adolescences have the advantage that many things are new and seemingly pose a challenge. Some may experience powerful emotions and thoughts that may hinder their emotional intelligence and ability to move forward. Yet most have less data from life experiences stored in their brains as memory; hence they are more apt to have words or events triggering chemical reactions and building brain cell growth and consequently sharper minds.

If we use our brains we will benefit from the "use it or lose it" syndrome. Young adolescents who actively learn new things—at school or at play or at home-- such as a new word, will trigger some reactions in the brain circuitry and the word will remain available – especially if we practice its use.

Young Adults

Young adults develop their memory and build their capacity to use their knowledge and memory and hence are less likely to lose them from inadequately challenging the brain circuitry. They are however more prone to re-experience some –if any—of their childhood fears and subsequent emotions that can stymie forward movement in their lives. Indeed young adults can experiences powerful emotions and thoughts that pull them in one direction or another and this may lead to some form of stress or other strong emotion such as love, anger or fear.

Building more balance and emotional intelligence helps these younger adults overcome constraints to brain cell growth— especially as they too are less burdened by large quantities of memories and comfortable patterns of behavior and more likely to seek out challenge and novelty provided they maintain their focus to stimulate the brain cell growth.

Middle Age

As we acquire more knowledge and skills and life experiences, perversely we run the greatest danger of inadequately challenging our Minds! We may be more tempted to stick with patterns or activities we prefer or know, and cruise along in comfort while perhaps our minds wander to other matters. It is when we think that something can be handled easily without undue attention and effort that run the risk of letting our minds slip.

Middle Age Plus

This issue of adapting a pattern of behavior that is comfortable and not seeking out challenges and new experiences can accelerate as we age. We may become more lax or our minds that are full of so much data may wander or we are just not quite so focused. In this situation we may find it harder to recall ort draw on our memory. However as we have acquired more life experience we may very well have also attained more balance and emotional intelligence so that our emotions and thoughts are more under our control, which dramatically improves our likelihood to keep our minds sharp.

It is vital to get out of the comfort zone—which can be the groups we socialize with or activities we do reasonably well- and face new things and new challenges that force us to concentrate and pay attention; is will keep us alert so that we notice more, help adjust our focus and help us master our emotions.

Consequently any re-organization by the brain that becomes solidified can have positive or negative impact on our lives. Positive effects mean that we are able to boost the functioning of our brains and benefit from better memories, better attention span and alertness; it can also have the effect of changing the brain circuitry positively so that people who have suffered strokes or loss of sight can develop their visual cortex to add sensitivity to their index fingers to boost their abilities to read Braille.

Once the changes are accepted as enduring by our malleable brains, reversing the modification is complicated and the alternative must be grooved into the brain like a skier forging another path through the deep snow.

Brain Quiz No. 2

What is the pattern? In this puzzle, three numbers: 16, 14, and 38, need to be assigned to one of the rows of numbers below. To which row should each number be assigned — A, B, or C?

A	0	6	8	9	3
B	5	13	2	10	16
C	7	1	47	11	17

Image 4: Brain Quiz 2

Chapter Three: Components of Emotional Intelligence

"People are like stained glass windows. They sparkle and shine when the sun is out, but when darkness sets in their true nature is revealed only if there is a light from within."
Elizabeth Kübler Ross

Emotional Intelligence is about seeking out what works and what is effective to ensure that we get what we want. Emotional Intelligence helps us get a better understanding of ourselves and others. It sets out a path towards quality personal self-knowledge, self-control, empathy and good relationships with oneself and others, which can significantly boost our abilities for personal and social satisfaction, chances of success, and sharper minds.

Intelligence Quotient (IQ) has been used as a surrogate of indicating intelligence but studies clearly show that IQ is unchangeable and actually is a less effective predictor of success, performance ability and popularity than Emotional Intelligence; moreover unlike our IQ Emotional Intelligence is more dynamic and we can develop it with expanded use.

We all face demands on our time and energy and using our Emotional Intelligence wisely can help us preserve a constructive approach to their deployment. The attachments we formed in our early years to parents or caregivers influence our preferred type of relationships and ways of communicating; yet EQ can be learned and as we acquire greater skills and competencies we can alter our initial preferences. With better knowledge of ourselves and greater understanding of others we can build relationships that better reflect our own needs and wants and meet those of others.

About Emotional Intelligence

Emotional Intelligence gives us multiple tools to examine our thoughts and emotions, how we can build more balance into our lives and how to gain more self-knowledge, manage our reactions, enhance our empathy and compassion and develop more effective relationships.

Emotional Intelligence is comprised of two sets of dimensions that are inextricably linked—with mutual impact. The outer ring deals with our range of feelings; whether we look inwardly or outwardly, our empathy and compassion and our balance between action, thoughts and wants. The inner ring delineates the four relationship strategies we all have available to us; even though we will have a preference to use one where others might also be appropriate. These options are: interdependent, independent, dependent, and dissociated. Our preferences are influenced by the earliest attachments we felt to parents or caregivers when we were young babies.

We can identify our Emotional Intelligence profile which is measured accurately online. To obtain our profile we watch a number of video clips and mark our responses to set questions that are put to us under simulated conditions of stress. This is tabulated and a computerized booklet is generated, which the client can discuss with the consultant to ascertain implications and connotations as well as discuss ways to develop any items of Emotional Intelligence that the client would like to develop. For more information contact the author who is a qualified Emotional Intelligence Consultant.

EMOTIONAL INTELLIGENCE

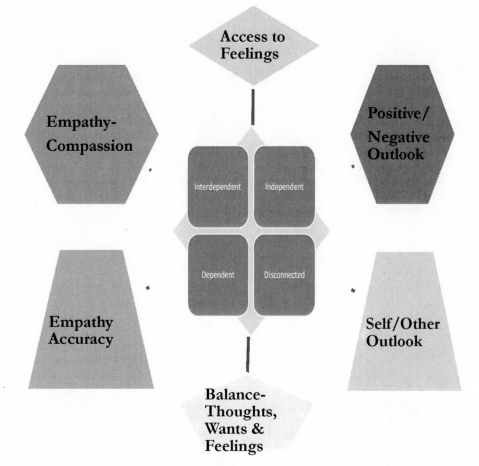

Image 5:- Components of Emotional Intelligence

Emotional Intelligence-Self Reflection and Empathy

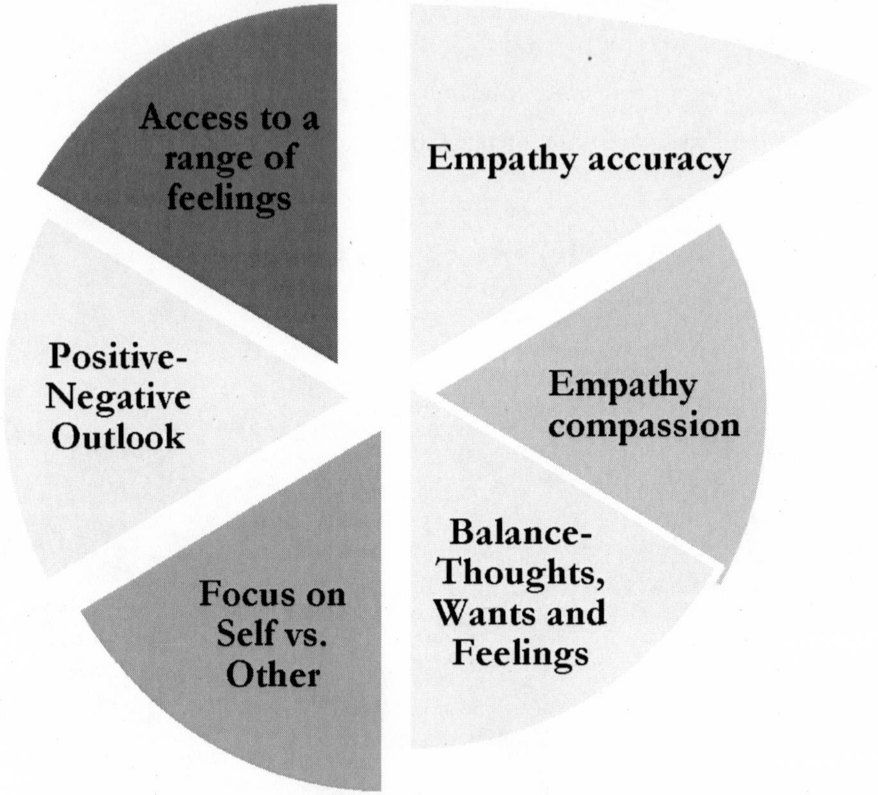

Image 6: EQ Self-Refection and Empathy

Components

Emotional Intelligence measures Self-Reflection and observation of self and the ability to be aware now of our present experience- as expressed by thoughts, feelings, and wants; plus the ability to differentiate ourselves from others and feel for them.

1. Access to a Range of Feelings

a. Having wide range of feelings and when to use them. These include all our emotions: - anger, joy, love, fear, sadness, anxiety and shame. This is valuable information for us to know as it heightens our understanding of ourselves and also of others; plus we can see if one or more are out of alignment.

b. It measures the breadth of feelings—not intensity. Feelings drive actions and the larger the palette of available feelings to us-especially when challenged- the easier it is to work with others.

2. Positive-Negative Outlook

a. The optimal blend is 75% positive and 25% negative.

b. It measures our optimism or negativity under stress; this can be our practical optimism while aware of real risks, or it can be a pre-disposition to see problems rather than opportunities.

3. Focus on Self or on Others

a. This measures how much we focus on ourselves, or how much our prime focus is on other. It examines where we get information—inside or outside; ideally we want a balance between them, which indicates self-respect and trust in our own experience and strengths, and how much we listen to others and honor their views.

b. It is the foundation of expanding our empathy and awareness of our power vis-à-vis others.

4. Balance—Thoughts, Wants and Feelings

a. These are the potential sources of our information. A balance implies that we get a wide range of information from our rational mind, our emotions and our desires as inputs to our brain.

b. For people who favor Thoughts: - are likely to be analytical, rational, good at problem-solving and more cautious.

c. For people who favor Wants: - are likely to be faster to action, get frustrated with those who are slower, may not analyze or consider feelings adequately, and use action as a substitute for emotional coping.

d. For those who favor Feelings: - are likely be aware of their feelings, but may get stuck or be blindsided by feelings and may not entirely rational.

5. Empathy—Accuracy

a. This is the ability to accurately describe another person's experience; it includes tuning into others and focusing on the other person and what that person is thinking and feeling. It also means making good "guesses" or assumptions about the other.

6. Empathy-Compassion

a. This is the ability to identify with another person's experience and "knowing" what it would be like to be that person; indeed it is the ability to "walk a mile in the other's shoes" and identify how that person thinks and feels.

A Sample Client's Computerized Chart

The following is a chart sample of what a client receives after having done the online test. No chart represents behavior, but it measures the internal experience of that client when under a degree of stress. See Image 7.

Sample Client's Emotional Intelligence Chart

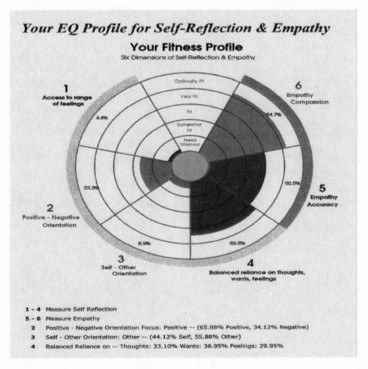

Image 7:- Client's EQ Self Reflection and Empathy Chart

Access to Feelings

This client seems to have difficulty connecting with her full range of feelings—particularly when challenged. Our emotions drive our actions, and consequently being able to connect with a wider range of emotions would give the client more vitality and heighten personal awareness and awareness of others. If the client has a questionable rating for access to feelings, this can be discussed with the Emotional Intelligence consultant and together they can work on developmental priorities depending on the client's circumstances, and the consultant might recommend some exercises to remediate where appropriate.

Positive-Negative Outlook

This client's focus is more negative than positive than that for most people. It suggests that when in a difficult situation this client is likely to interpret the situation negatively. Such a client could experience impatience, anger, and anxiety and possibly intolerance for self or others. A healthy practice would be to notice positive thoughts and feelings and when the client is disposed to judge others; then she could see any pitfalls more clearly and suggest what is right rather than veer to describing what is wrong.

Self-Other Outlook

The ratings here suggest that this client has a tendency to take her cue from the other rather than focusing on her own experience. She may feel that other people are in control and is very sensitive to feedback. It is very helpful for this client to perceive feedback as information and not criticism.

Balance- Feelings, Thoughts and Wants

This client has a good balance; it means she can move between her feelings, thoughts and wants with ease, which generally means she can understand and communicate with a wide variety of people, and others find her easy to approach.

Empathy-Accuracy

The client seems to be accurately attuned to others and perceives what they are experiencing, and is able to take in a person's verbal and non-verbal behavior easily; also she seems to be able to make pretty good assessments of what they may be experiencing. There is still some risk that the client does not always check that her observations are accurate.

Empathy-Compassion

This client has an excellent ability to emotionally identify with others and what they are experiencing; this implies she can sufficiently manage her own feelings so that she can genuinely listen to another, and thus be viewed as supportive.

Relationship Strategies

The inner ring of figure of Emotional Intelligence chart on page denotes the four relationship strategies we can use to control our actions and reactions.

We all develop in Relationships; moreover we have relationships with everyone and thing we encounter—the term is not just reserved for our connection with our special other! Relationships are an integral part of Emotional Intelligence as not only do our brains develop in relationship, but so too do our emotional competencies which continue throughout our lifetimes. This developmental approach to Emotional Intelligence is based on the attachment theories outlined by Dr Daniel Siegel, in his (1999) book " The Developing Mind"; in which he states our default choice of relationship strategy is influenced by genetics and environment- notably by our early parental or caretaker environment that had a huge impact on very young neural pathways. These early influences impact the way we perceive the world (our Weltanschauung) as well as our communication patterns and levels of trust.

Four Relationship Strategies

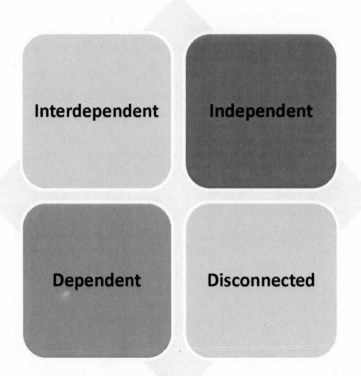

Image 8:- Relationship Strategies

Research shows that a child learns by acquiring skills, building competencies-both intrapersonal such as accurate self-assessment and interpersonal, such as communication, conflict management, and learns to differentiate the self from others, and to control own impulses and learns empathy. These are building blocks for Emotional Intelligence that we can develop throughout our lives.

There are four basic ways we attach to our parents or caregivers-depending on circumstances. This attachment is based on the parent's sensitivity and response level to the child's signals; studies show that this pattern is established in the first year of the child's life. A child will only attach to a few people as a way of seeking protection from external threat, and the child tends to mirror the perceptions of the parent or caregiver.

While the attachment may be clumsy at the beginning it gradually becomes less so as the child's muscular coordination and attachment proclivities develop. The child absorbs the pattern of emotional communication and establishes meaning and values linked to those very early social interactions. Hence the pattern of attachment also determines the child's preference for communication and relationship strategies with other people.

These patterns are established from very early years and as they are repeated by the parent or caregiver they become encoded and form part of the child's expectations of the world. While these are created from an early age, we all can change and modify each of these aspects by promoting out Emotional Intelligence development.

SECURE

Where the parents are sensitive to the child's signals; their can amplify child's positive emotions or counteract negative ones. Mutual rhythm and this builds a stronger reflective aspect for the child; who feels secure and can self soothe or cope with distressing circumstances.

AVOIDANT

Parent is emotionally less available and less responsive to the child; so limited responsive communication. Reflective function is not well developed in the child due to parental lack of guidance; child develops personal techniques for self-soothing and is more self reliant, and isolationist.

AMBIVALENT

Parent is inconsistent in their communication with mixed messages and unresponsive to the rhythm of the child; which child experiences as intrusive or off-kilter. Child may not feel secure, with inadequate self-soothing skills, and play and social interaction will be impaired. Child may use approach-withdrawal.

DISCONNECTED

Parents' actions, thoughts and feelings are inconsistent and lack cohesion:- so child has fragmented and inconsistent patterns of thoughts, feelings or actions. Ability of child to reflect is greatly impaired, and may have great difficulty in being coherent under stress; feel risk of threat or separation and may have disjointed speech.

Image 9:- Four Types of Attachments

Relationship Strategies

All relationship strategies have value. We need to vary our use of each according to circumstances and our level of trust even though we will tend towards one and use it more often than warranted due to the kind of attachment we had with our parents or caregiver.

Ideally we should select the appropriate relationship strategy to meet the situation, despite our inner preferences.

There are times when it is desirable to function in an interdependent way; this is highly collaborative. Other times it is more effective to be more independent—especially if one works alone or we know we will have to take authority and make decisions for others; other times it is more useful to cede authority to another and use the dependent strategy. Finally there may be times when it is more appropriate to leave the relationship entirely, either emotionally or also physically, as it is not going anywhere; in short we are simply wasting our time and energy by perpetuating the relationship.

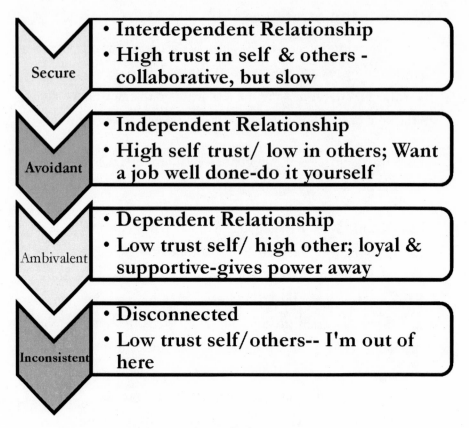

Image 10:- Preferred Relationship Strategies and Attachments

Trust

A major variant between these strategies is the level of trust—both in oneself and in the other, and there are a number of exercises that help build that trust level.

Our emotions guide our interpretation of ourselves, our world and the choices we make. With a greater sense of security we are more open to trust and take risks and participate fully in relationships. With a lesser sense of security we lose trust and tend to pull away to protect ourselves.

We can build trust by noticing the level of need we have in the relationship in order to achieve high priority goals; if that need is less than we previously thought we can reduce our level of distrust. Moreover we can build higher trust by practicing conversations. The interdependent relationship strategy depends on high level of trust-both of self and the other. It is a collaborative approach and uses open and direct communication; it is often linked to a positive orientation, empathy compassion, good listening skills and an environment that encourages individual contributions.

More specifically we can build trust in others by acknowledging the other person, having self-trust and having a commitment to be engaged and be actively involved in the relationship while maintaining personal honesty and integrity. It helps also to notice what is essential for you to feel trust in another, and ask for feedback about how your trust affects the other.

This is used by individuals with high self-trust but low trust in others; it is good for going it alone and taking charge, making difficult decisions and handling resistance. It is often used by risk-takers or can serve as a powerful antidote to organizational anxiety! Although it can be highly effective it does have the disadvantage that it discourages interactions with others and sometimes that is valuable for a sense of belonging.

Thirdly—but still in many ways the starting point, we must have trust in ourselves as this helps us participate fully in relationships without giving away our personal power or sparkle. Here self-refection can support self-trust, as well as journaling, noticing your right to count and be part of the now and that you make a valid contribution.

Valuing relationships is primary characteristic of this strategy. Individuals who use this strategy seek out relationship and are willing to cede authority and be loyal and more vulnerable in the relationship. It works very well when dealing with competent people and where participative management is encouraged. However, individuals need to watch out for falling prey to self-doubt or giving away too much personal power and avoiding dealing with resistance.

In cases where trust is very low the individual may have difficulty in coping or be viewed as clinging. Here the person may also lose self-faith and may physically drop the relationship which could be the best option if remediation does not work.

Brain Quiz No. 3

Count the number of times that the letter F appears in the following sentence:

"Finished files are the result of years of scientific study combined with the experience of years"

Chapter 4: Emotional Intelligence-Implications

"Life shrinks or expands in proportion to one's courage."
Anais Nin

I. Emotional Intelligence and Relationships

The great thing about Emotional Intelligence is that it is dynamic and we can learn more and more and expand our own Emotional Intelligence, and consequently change our behaviors. The early years do have a big impact on our relationships and styles of communication but they are not set in concrete and we can alter them as we learn more about Emotional Intelligence.

Children exposed to each of these attachment styles will tend to prefer associated relationship strategies as indicated in Image 15. The implication being that although children will use all relationship strategies they may rely on their preferences more often than optimally effective.

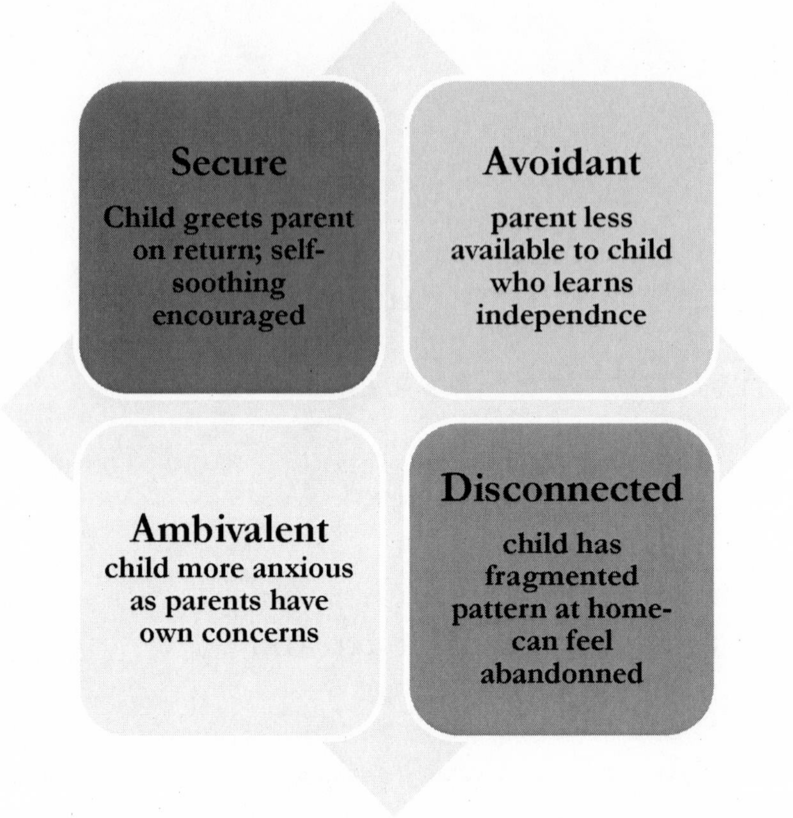

Secure
Child greets parent on return; self-soothing encouraged

Avoidant
parent less available to child who learns independnce

Ambivalent
child more anxious as parents have own concerns

Disconnected
child has fragmented pattern at home-can feel abandonned

Image 11:- Attachment Styles

Getting to know one's attachment preference and the uses of each relationship strategy are part of boosting Emotional Intelligence and we are capable of altering our patterns of relationship—whether at work or at home with our spouse and family or with other non-work connections. A key way to do this is to examine our level of trust. We build trust by keeping our commitments with integrity, and if we look at the impact our decision-making style has on others and to ourselves as it is easy to swing from autocratic decision-making to consensual decision-making, and each has its own appropriate situation.

Frequently the issue may be related to trusting others and this requires us first to build trust in ourselves and then in others. For this it helps to isolate what is essential to you to feel trust; it is often gained from clear and honest statements at the outset about your intentions for the interaction, and then *listen* actively to the responses; making it clear that you have paid attention to what was said. If we lack trust we are unlikely to delegate; so take it back a step and express your concerns about the "other" with clarity and respect, and then move forward.

Building trust in ourselves is the essence of trust; it involves believing our own feelings and emotions and being able to control them. As we learn to become more aware and value our own experiences we gain sensitivity to our thoughts and feelings and we are able to build a picture of positive versus destructive messages we have heard and from whom. It helps to practice looking at what we are feeling or thinking now—in the present moment. As we focus on what is going on around us and how we feel, we are able to switch off our ever- present judgment switch and still our internal chatter.

When we alter one relationship, all will come under question, and we can review how we best would like to be effective in that situation.

Relationship Strategies and Communication Styles

Our patterns of communication are also heavily influenced by our initial attachments. Emotions are at the root of everything we do and guide our interpretation of ourselves, our world and our choices.

We, as children begin the process to calm ourselves by learning ways to reconcile our emotions and settle ourselves; this is aided by the input we get from our earliest relationships. We do develop preferred forms of communication based on that earliest relationship, which we resort to more easily when under stress, although once we become more aware of these factors we are able to modify them through raising our level of Emotional Intelligence development.

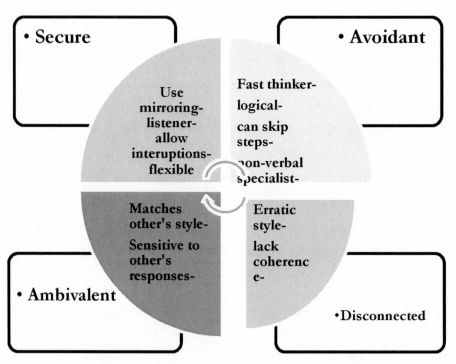

Image 12:- Communication Styles by Attachment Types

Relationship Development as Adults

Building trust helps us develop our Emotional Intelligence as we gain experiences and provides us with more options for the varied strategies. Experience does not alter the fact that we deal with emotions-whether we want to or not- they are part of us; and if we do not recognize them we are putting on blinkers to some part of who we are in this universe. We store every single emotion in our brain that we can retrieve at will. Failure to recognize the emotion we are experiencing will distort our brain's filing system and make retrieval or remembering much harder.

All emotional data is stored in the amygdala, and with greater development of our Emotional Intelligence we improve our cataloguing capabilities and thereby boost the speed and efficiency of the data retrieval or remembering.

II. Emotional Intelligence and Emotions

Relationships are vital to our development and influenced by our basic emotions. We need our emotions to learn about the world and about ourselves. They are intrinsically human and we cannot escape them. In Emotional Intelligence we realize that we have a palette of basic emotions and appreciating the nature of these feelings helps us know ourselves better and reclaim our soul.

There are situations where certain emotions become more dominant and they can take on a disproportionate relevance to us, which cause our brains to close down the cellular growth and cloud our thinking that can become rigid and even prompt inaction. This is not a good time to make important decisions. The emotions that fluctuate wildly in both directions are: anger, anxiety, fear, love, joy, sadness and shame; these emotions can, according to research by Kevin Ochsner, be reined in using the following strategies.

Strategies for Curbing Great Fluctuations of Emotions

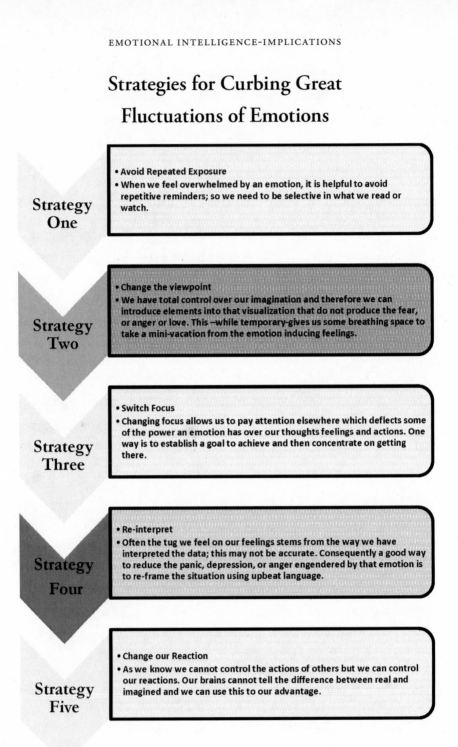

Strategy One
- Avoid Repeated Exposure
- When we feel overwhelmed by an emotion, it is helpful to avoid repetitive reminders; so we need to be selective in what we read or watch.

Strategy Two
- Change the viewpoint
- We have total control over our imagination and therefore we can introduce elements into that visualization that do not produce the fear, or anger or love. This –while temporary-gives us some breathing space to take a mini-vacation from the emotion inducing feelings.

Strategy Three
- Switch Focus
- Changing focus allows us to pay attention elsewhere which deflects some of the power an emotion has over our thoughts feelings and actions. One way is to establish a goal to achieve and then concentrate on getting there.

Strategy Four
- Re-interpret
- Often the tug we feel on our feelings stems from the way we have interpreted the data; this may not be accurate. Consequently a good way to reduce the panic, depression, or anger engendered by that emotion is to re-frame the situation using upbeat language.

Strategy Five
- Change our Reaction
- As we know we cannot control the actions of others but we can control our reactions. Our brains cannot tell the difference between real and imagined and we can use this to our advantage.

Image 13:- Strategies for Curbing Wide Changes in Emotions

Emotions that Can Fluctuate Widely

Stress

- We all feel stress at some point in our lives and at times it can become intense. It often combines with other emotions such as; fear, anger, and anxiety. Switching focus and avoid repetition help us regain more control when under stress. Yet if stress gets out of hand it can have a negative impact on our brain's ability to grow, and key chemicals no longer stimulate brain cell growth –indeed they can have the opposite effect and reduce our motivation to exercise and look after ourselves.

Fear

- Fear is quite widespread and is often linked with stress. It incorporates apprehension, anxiety, distress, dread, fright, horror, panic, shock, overwhelmed, and worry. All the above strategies can alleviate this unpleasant feeling; one especially useful one is reinterpreting the data.

Anxiety

- This is a natural reaction to a threat, whether real or perceived. If left untended it can lead to "panic" attacks. All strategies can help alleviate this emotion.

Anger

- This can be set off by events such as loss of power or status, the theft of something we value, receiving insults or not having our expectations met. It often brings us pain- either to ourselves or to others. Sometimes we have a sense that we have not been treated fairly and that others do not understand. All five strategies assist us in coming to terms with this emotion.

Love

- A powerful emotion, and while we generally think of it positively, it too can alter the chemical levels in our brain, and that can radically change how we act and react. While seemingly positive all five strategies at differing times can assist us regain more balance as this emotion can diminish our power to reason and it can blind us to logic as well as limit our powers of differentiation and judgment so that at times we feel out of control.

III. Emotional Intelligence and Implications for Thinking

Our thinking significantly contributes to our Emotional Intelligence; this is the way we make sense of the world in a rational way, and we interpret it in ways that are significant to our needs, beliefs, objectives and values that often mold and are influenced by our emotions. We all think. But not necessarily in the same way –even though logic is the dominant force here.

Difference between Thinking and Feeling

Our thoughts are logical and follow patterns of rationality; whereas our feelings are more ethereal and represent our basic emotions. They are stored in different parts of the brain. The amygdala stores every emotion we have ever experienced, and thoughts are stored in the neocortex.

Thoughts and feelings are often confused as we may say "I feel tired" giving the impression that this thought is a feeling. Another example would be a young girl is bitten by a dog, and her thoughts could be: that hurts, get that dog away from me, but her feelings would be I am afraid of dogs or I feel anxious of that dog. In this example, the young girl has stored the memory of the dog bite and if she sees another dog her amygdala in her brain triggers a chemical reaction of fear or anxiety. Whereas her rational neocortex will trigger a more logical thought not to get too close to a dog.

There is a strong link between feelings and thoughts, and generally we will experience a feeling that prompts a thought; the thought triggers an action that has a consequence, and this prompts another feeling, which in turn produces a thought and so on.

This is represented in the following chart.

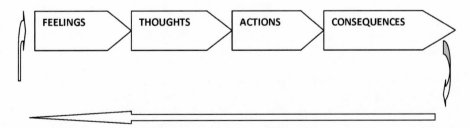

Image 14:- Emotions-Thoughts-Action-Sequence

We can chart these events putting in each step of our own issue, and then we can review where we might have changed the thought to produce a different action and consequence. Evidence supports the fact that if we change the thought –which has an underlying rational- we will change the action and how the event evolves. It is easier to change the thought than the feeling, although that too can be achieved using our Emotional Intelligence and techniques.

We may also realize that the bulk of our thoughts are circular and keep percolating in our heads- so thinking has limits and change can be beneficial.

Emotional Intelligence can Transform Thoughts

Who would we be without our thoughts?

It is our thoughts that cause suffering in the world. By examining them we can identify the real cause of our problems, and perceive what is hurting us. The circular thinking means we can become prisoners of that same old story!

Thoughts use a lot of energy. Consequently we must make sure that they are in tune with reality and not projections of how I "should" behave- especially when someone else decides what that "should" be.

We are responsible for our own thoughts and reactions and there is nobody else is forcing them on us. They can cause pain and as thought specialist, Byron Katie, said:

"I discovered that when I believed my thoughts, I

suffered; but when I didn't believe them, I did not suffer, and that is true for every human being. Freedom is as simple as that. I found suffering is optional. I found joy within me that has never disappeared- not for a single moment. That joy is in everyone, always."

How we perceive ourselves and what we believe is the thrust of our story. Everything has cause and effect. What has happened to us, even if only partially remembered, has its effect on how we act. It is at times like this that we can slow down and ask ourselves: "who would we be without that thought?"

A thought is worthless unless we give it meaning and believe it; moreover we frequently attach an image to that thought, and this may well be an illusion. Indeed, as we cannot prove the existence of the image it does not exist. So we get go into self-imposed contortions over a representation that we have created in our imagination.

What do we do to break this pattern of thinking that causes so much pain? Byron Katie, now a world leader in the mastery of thought, went through her own learning process and concludes that we must start by examining the thoughts more carefully. She proposes that we investigate each situation by asking her four questions:-

   i.   Is it true?
   ii.   How can I know it is really true?
   iii.   How do I react with the thought?
   iv.   Who would I be without this thought?

To simplify the process, Byron Katie, provides worksheets that are available at her website (www.thework.com); this has a number of questions about anyone who is causing us stress or hurt. If you do not have the worksheet you can write about the situation and person causing the hurt. Then pose each of the four questions above. Sometimes if we are going to deepen our knowledge it will take a little while to allow the true answer to come to us; it is about opening our hearts and not trying to change our thoughts here.

An example, might be a friend Max who has started to see Carol, and spends time and money on her; he tells me not to feel jealous.

- Do I believe this to be true? Yes.
- Is it absolutely true? No because he still calls for a walk with the dogs occasionally.
- How do I react when I think the jealous thought? I lose my appetite, blame myself and feel anxious.
- What would I be without this thought? Less victimized and more at peace with myself.

It helps us make our thinking explicit and permits us to gain a better awareness and perspective, and ensure that these are actually our thoughts and not those borrowed from a cleric, friend or TV show.

Changing our Thinking-the Turnaround

Then Byron Katie proposes that we turn the statements around and look at the alternatives. There are three basic turnarounds, and some or all may apply. These include:-

a. Switching the thought expressed to cover oneself instead of the other party.

b. Switching to mean the opposite.

c. Or switching around to apply to others or change the subject of the sentence.

For instance:-

Under a) "Paul doesn't understand me" turns around to "I do not understand myself".

Under b) it becomes "Paul does understand me".

Under c) it becomes "I don't understand Paul".

We want to allow ourselves to think these through and with an open mind we can come up with alternatives that ring true for us. It is a fine way to check whether our stories are real and valid and gives us a chance to experience the opposite. We so often craft stories and identities that are based on selective recall which can distort the picture.

Byron Katie points out that it is easy to confuse areas that we can control with those we can't. In times of stress and loss we tend to opt for stories that fit our selective thoughts and frequently blame ourselves into the bargain. By focusing on taking care of my business, we are able to relieve a lot of self-blandishment, depression and isolation. It is not easy. Yet practicing the investigative tools and working on the turnarounds help us lessen the anxiety and find more peace. The more we see ourselves as we truly are, the more we grow with Emotional Intelligence and act with sharper minds.

Brain Quiz No. 4

Image 21:- Two Puppies

Look at both puppies—both are identical. A closely monitored, scientific study revealed that, in spite of the fact that the puppies are identical, if under stress a person would find differences between the two puppies.

Chapter Five: Use of Sharp Minds with Emotional Intelligence-Communication

"Experience is <u>not</u> what happens to you, it's what you do with what happens to you."
Aldous Huxley.

Emotional Intelligence and Sharper Minds

When we develop our Emotional Intelligence we are able to boost our perceptions, decision-making facilities, our empathy and our abilities to react accurately and our ability to choose an appropriate relationship strategy. In particular we are in better control of our emotions and thoughts that allow us make certain that the cellular growth in our brains is positive and we benefit from having sharper minds.

In this way we are better able to:-

o   Access a wide range of feelings and be able to identify what we are experiencing; which provides us with valuable information on how to interact with others.

o   We will have a healthy blend of being able to see the positive and negative aspects of a situation and interaction and with this focus you will not get stuck in despair.

o   We will have a good blend between what we want for ourselves and for others and will take feedback as information rather than criticism and will not give excessive power to another.

o   We will have a balance in our sources of information and not rely too heavily on any of them; this means you can factor in rational thought and your emotions as well as what you want which gives you valuable information and boosts your ability to handle turbulent relationships.

o   We can accurately tune into others and understand what they are experiencing; this involves being able to read both verbal and non-verbal communication and correctly assume the thoughts feeling and wants of others.

o   We have a well developed ability to join others in knowing what their experiences must be like—even if this is not always comfortable we can "walk a mile in their shoes".

o   We have an ability to choose the appropriate relationship strategy depending on context and type of relationship.

   •   This demonstrates flexibility and versatility; so at times we can operate in a highly collaborative interdependent way,

   •   or in other situations we can move with independence and take authority as appropriate,

   •   or in other circumstances we can give authority to others and be loyal and dependent,

   •   or at times we can have the wisdom to quit if this is essential to maintaining a healthy relationship.

Uses for Communication

One of the key aspects of Emotional Intelligence is that it helps us improve the way we communicate and our ability to take in information, process it accurately and respond succinctly.

Communication includes speaking or writing what's on our mind and therefore requires us to know our minds, a decision about what we want to achieve, and know what forms of communication to use, the feedback and our response and how to measure our success.

The importance of communication has proliferated in the 21 st century and is vital to our daily living and success in everything we do. We spend about 80% of our time communicating in one way or another; hence advancing this skill is a major facet of the importance of Emotional Intelligence in our lives.

Causes of Misunderstandings

We do have different modes of thinking and reasoning as our perceptions will vary according to our cultural, ethnic, social backgrounds and differing religious upbringings and values. Moreover, in some cultures we say what we mean explicitly whereas in other cultures the context affects the meaning greatly and the communication can be less explicit.

Gender too plays a role according to by Dr. Marianne Legato (2005) who considers men and women think differently and use different filters to emphasize their point, and Dr Legato contends that men are more task-oriented while women use more non-verbal forms of communication for emphasis.

Additionally, misunderstandings are accentuated by the differing interpretations and uses of non-verbal communications and gestures that may mean one thing in one culture but may have a different, or zero, meaning in another.

How does Communication Work?

The sender encodes a message—either verbally using words or non-verbally using gestures or body expressions. The meanings are generally but not automatically understood; they are transmitted by phone, direct face-to-face speech, in written materials including by email. The message is then decoded by receiver, who may start the loop again by giving feedback or encoding another message back. At each point there is room for inaccuracies to creep in. Effective communication will avoid ambiguity and be as clear and concise as possible, but what is direct and sincere to one culture may appear brash and rude in another.

Non-Verbal Communication

Non-verbal forms of communication tend to reflect underlying feelings and are often used to clarify or emphasize a point, denote when one has finished speaking, point out a contradiction, and reveal a person's true feelings about a topic.

The use of gestures, facial expressions, body language and posture are all part of non-verbal forms of communication, which have communicative value; yet they do not all mean the same thing. For instance, there are seven emotions conveyed by facial expressions, and their meaning varies. Likewise there are different meanings for the way we stand, walk, or sit, and huge differences in how we handle and tolerate touch and physical closeness. Indeed there are over 700,000 non-verbals –ranging from body movements, voice qualifiers, the way we dress, approaches to time or to material possessions, accents, age or gender.

Perception is Selective

We screen out information to avoid overload simply due to the volume of data flowing back and forth; which implies we develop selective perception. That perception, once we have it established becomes the way we tend to view things—even if it is inaccurate. It can be more accurate and mindful if we use our Emotional intelligence to listen actively and by the use of our empathy skills.

Emotional Intelligence Helps us be Good Listeners

Listening and hearing are not the same. Just because someone can hear and make the passive act of perceiving sound, that does not mean that the words are being interpreted and understood which is the core of effective listening.

For active listening we need to shut out our thoughts, overcome outside distractions, avoid day-dreaming, avoid interruptions with our questions, not rehearse our answers, or over rely on high-tech devices as none are substitutes for paying attention. As listeners we also face the dilemma that on average most of us prefer speaking to listening. Yet people do want to be heard, and this is a necessary skill for well rounded communicator.

Improving Listening Skills

Research indicates that there is a major listening gap, and we only listen efficiently 25 % of the time. Simple ways to improve our listening is to do so with a purpose, checking our understanding by paraphrasing, avoiding any distractions, and neutralizing snap judgments. In this way we devote our full attention to the speaker. It does take concentration but is highly effective.

Good Communication

How we communicate is critical to the way we live and lead our lives. Deep down we all have a need to share our basic thoughts, ideas, as well as how we feel and what are our main beliefs. We may not always feel comfortable in sharing these things with all comers—especially in the work environment, but we all develop techniques to share in a way that we view as appropriate to the international dimensions of our cultural environment.

Underpinning all relationships is the need for mutual understanding. Communication serves four main functions:-

- Control—we can use tricks and tools that clarify what we are doing; these can include some sort of guidelines which allow feedback;
- Motivation—we can encourage others and show our appreciation;
- Emotional expression—depending on the situation we can show feelings or ways of promoting social solidarity;
- Transfer information—we can pass on and receive back valuable information.

Emotional Intelligence improves our communication abilities as we become more aware of ourselves and of the people with whom we are communicating, as well as the kind of relationship strategy we want to deploy for our selected form of communication.

Brain Quiz No. 5

Light Bulb Puzzle

There are three switches in Room A

Each corresponds to three light bulbs in Room B

You can turn the switches on and off
and leave them in any position

You are only allowed one trip to Room B

How would you identify which switch
corresponds to each light bulb?

Chapter Six: Use of Sharp Minds with Emotional Intelligence-Relationships

"It's a funny thing about life, if you refuse to accept anything but the best, you very often get it."
Somerset Maugham

The ability to manage ourselves effectively in relationships—especially challenging ones- requires an ability to quieten aroused distresses so that we can stay in that relationship. The prime requirement is trust; for which we need a sense of safety so that we are honest with ourselves and with others.

Trust is something we learn and practice through our relationships. By being aware of our own emotions and those of others we can learn to increase our levels of trust to manage relationships effectively. So how can we alter our trust?

As Dr. Ron Short states, it is by boosting our Emotional Intelligence that allows us to shape and sustain successful relationships in today's environment. EQ facilitates more internal balance that enables a more harmonious approach, both with oneself and also with others; this is complemented by our use of accurate empathy and compassionate empathy.

As we highlighted earlier, accurate empathy is being able to correctly interpret the other person; compassion is about getting people do things by making sure they want to do them. It starts with listening and demonstrates a deep understanding of the other person's hopes and dreams as well as trust in them and oneself.

All too often the pressures of daily living means that that we can sacrifice our values and priorities to external obligations. We may feel compelled to act in a certain way by our organization, or by the pressure we face to perform and produce results. Moreover, we expect the same of others. We may think that unsuccessful relationships are the result of the environment or mistakes by others. Under stress we tend to see the world in black and white terms.

This leads us to blame others if things go wrong and feel sorry for ourselves. As a consequence, we may get depressed or find coping mechanisms with painkillers, drink, drugs or food. One frequent outcome can be poorer performance, or it may have damaging health effects and increase anxiety, nervousness and stress. It can lead to burn-out and a sense that we are out of control in our relationships.

With greater Emotional Intelligence we manage our own emotions, expand our empathy and compassion so that we have a better vision of people and who they are and what they are experiencing. Emotional intelligence fosters our ability to interact with integrity so that we build trust and in the process sharpen our minds.

Why are Relationships Important to Us?

We seek relationships for dialogue and learning, to play with others, to share humor, to learn using mutual inquiry, to collaborate with others, or to blame others.

The relationship can be primarily about oneself and may be to celebrate or even berate oneself, or it could be about someone else with the prime goal is to seek solace, undermine the other, or to set boundaries to create or avert conflict.

Emotional Intelligence equips us with tools to move from being an average to an excellent leader. EQ is about developing self-awareness and the ability to manage own emotions, and social competencies to build strong trusting relationships, demonstrate empathy, and non-fear means to motivate.

A key ingredient of EQ involves understanding and appreciating the uses of the four relationship strategies. This is particularly pertinent as we need to handle the changes of our fast paced globalized economy and information revolution. We require these strategies for all the relationships we have in our lives- personal with our families and special other, with our friends, with our social, spiritual, and philanthropic, groups, and work. There are many types of relationships. Each involves social, mental and physical activities that trigger activation for sharper minds. Emotional Intelligence vastly increases our abilities to boost our Brain Fitness and do well in our relationships.

Personal Relationships

Our non-work relationships often set the tone for our work ones. How we interact with our boss, colleagues or business associates and in our various groups can be molded by the environment, but gradually they will mirror the relationships we have at home and in our personal lives. Most of us have an idea of what kind of personal relationship we imagine a "good" or "correct" relationship should represent. We can cause ourselves needless distress by comparing our own relationships with the idea of what a relationship "should be like" and then concluding, by comparison, ours is defective.

Transference from Initial Attachment

Most relationships tend to copy our initial relationship with our parents or caregiver. This important early relationship is often with someone we trusted or who influenced us greatly—such as a parent, a teacher or therapist. In this way we notice how that person behaves and we imitate those ways with others in our lives. This can include correct or mistaken attributions; moreover this static approach can be entirely inappropriate later in life with other people we encounter and may even prove counterproductive.

Trust in ourselves as well as the other is a mark of Emotional Intelligence. It gives us the wisdom to choose partners –in both personal, in group and work relationships- and help us meet our needs, grow by setting reasonable boundaries, expand our tolerance, take more control over our emotions, validate our feelings and thoughts, be more aware of ourselves and others, and know whether the relationship is a good fit or not.

Social and Work Groups

Relationships in all social or work groups essentially will reflect our personal relationships, and we will face a slightly different environment that can bring out other traits. Groups can be socially, spiritually, philanthropically oriented, and will involve a group dynamic. This is one of the reasons why social interaction is viewed as an important element in the human activities needed to induce the chemical reaction that triggers Brain Fitness.

So not only are social interactions, whether at work or not, vital for our progress to Brain Fitness, they are deeply impacted by our Emotional Intelligence. They vastly improve our self-awareness and appreciation of others so that our relationships are enhanced and we manage ourselves more efficiently to avoid wasting time and effort.

Group Dynamics

We all deal with multiple group dynamics. Groups we join tend to align with our interests and needs. An obvious example is our work environment where we interact with our portion of the hierarchy and also with our customers, clients, suppliers and support people. In the course of our work we will, undoubtedly, attend a huge number of meetings- indeed approximately 11 million meetings are held every day in the USA. Relly Nadler (2007), who has consulted widely and written a book on Leadership, emphasizes the importance of clarifying a meeting's purpose at the outset, and keeping it on track. Is this a regular Monday morning meeting, or an information gathering meeting, or another type? Much can be deduced from those invited and the agenda- if one exists. Often politics will play a significant role. In one-on-one meetings it is more difficult to set a precise agenda –especially as it may touch on emotional or unpredictable issues.

Having a clear idea of the direction we want will help deflect going astray by tangents at meetings and, thus, failing to achieve the desired goal. Acquiring mastery at meetings- both social and at work - tend to break down complicated concepts into their most basic forms and any misunderstandings can be deflected *en route*. Most groups will have a meeting menace, or a troublemaker. This may be due to a lack of effective listening skills, a person's preference to be in the limelight and be the talker rather than the listener, or due to disregard for cultural differences.

The impact can be limited by acting with Emotional Intelligence that curbs run-away emotions and thoughts, shows greater self-awareness and respect for the other's perspective and shows appropriate choice of relationship strategies for each situation and person.

By curbing and managing one's emotions and acting with a greater balance so that feelings and thoughts are synchronized and actions are well considered and not imposed on the group, the group dynamic can be a catalyst for change and growth. With improved EQ we can more easily handle the challenges of group dynamics and handle relationships with greater leadership skills.

Brain Quiz No. 6

7	4	8
3	9	7
6	5	10
?	8	4

Image 16:- Missing Number

Work out the pattern here and insert the missing number.

Chapter Seven: Emotional Intelligence and Leadership

*"Sooner or later, those who win are
those who think they can."*
Richard Bach

Ironically the first task in leadership has nothing to do with leading others, but knowing and managing ourselves. As David Gergen, senior political analyst and adviser to four US Presidents, said, "Emotional Intelligence and emotions are at the heart of effective leadership". This involves connecting with one's deep values, beliefs and culture. This process then enables us to recognize our emotions and tune into those of others as we align our emotions with our goals.

Image 17:- Follow my Lead

Leadership, whether at work, social groups or at home, is about coping with change, and envisaging a direction and getting the support of others to follow our guidance and allow others to be the best they can be. This uses motivational, communication and relationship skills that we can boost using Emotional Intelligence.

Qualities that boost leadership abilities are frequently considered to consist primarily of intelligence (as measured by IQ ratings), toughness, determination, and vision, but research by people like Daniel Goleman and Richard Boyatzis show that while IQ and technical skills are important as basic threshold factors, the main determinant of effective leadership is Emotional Intelligence.

Goleman was the first to uncover direct ties between measurable positive results of success and the dimensions of Emotional Intelligence—awareness of emotions, ability to name thoughts and feelings and differentiate our feelings from those of others, self-regulation using relationship strategies to regulate our emotions and empathy with another's experience. Indeed, his research goes on to indicate that a person with greater responsibility has a stronger need for Emotional Intelligence in order to be effective.

It is not simply a matter of charisma, but involves a set of Emotional Intelligence skills that can be learned. With these skills as Daniel Goleman's (1998) research shows 40% of employees are unable to take criticism without reacting with hostility. With better Emotional Intelligence skills people are able to communicate clearly, motivate and overcome resistance to change.

The starting point is to boost self awareness and self knowledge, without which we limit our vision and resistance to change thereby limiting effective team work. It means having a deep understanding of one's emotions and their relative strengths and areas that need development which allows the individual to have a realistic and honest self-awareness. In this way each person can recognize how their feelings affect them, other people, and their job performance. Such an individual is comfortable talking candidly-including personal limitations and strengths.

With Emotional Intelligence we learn to become more aware of our feelings, the range of feeling, and how others are feeling and react; moreover we are able to achieve a more viable balance within ourselves that inspires others. Effective leaders are able to radiate positive thoughts and ignite positive emotions around them. Understanding one's emotions helps us act with integrity in reliable and adaptable ways and with flexibility. It is the ability to recognize and understand our moods, emotions, and drives, as well as their effect on others; it is evident by self-confidence, realistic self-assessment and a keen sense of humor. Knowing oneself is a necessary prelude to being able to assess others.

We are emotional beings and although we cannot eliminate our feelings, we can manage ourselves in challenging relationships. The four relationship strategies vary according to the level of trust we have in ourselves and with others.

Self –regulation is the ability to control or redirect disruptive impulses and moods and think before acting; it is characterized by trustworthiness and integrity, comfort with ambiguity and openness to change. This creates an environment that is reasonable and fair. It enables the individual to adapt to ambiguity and change so that the individual is able to reflect and suspend judgment, gather more information, and listen before adopting a different relationship strategy.

Of all the dimensions of emotional intelligence, empathy is the most easily recognized. We have all felt the empathy of a sensitive friend, and we have experienced what it is like when it is absent. It includes both accuracy for what the other is feeling and compassion by understanding what that is like. It is indicative of a wise person in today's environment where teams are vital, technology and globalization brings closer communication and it attracts and retains talent. People tend to be very effective at managing relationships when they can understand and control their own emotions and can empathize with the feelings of others.

It is fortunate, then, that emotional intelligence can be learned. Individuals learn to how to leverage these skills to optimize their performance and that of their team and achieve leadership success and behave more mindfully and wisely.

Brain Quiz No. 7

Image 18:- Cake Cutting

How do you cut a cake into eight equal
pieces with only three cuts?

[Not necessarily identical cake]

Chapter Eight: Age Proof your Brain--Q & A

Coincidence is a messenger sent by truth.
-Jacqueline Winspear

Here are some of your questions with my answers:-

Why is Emotional Intelligence Important?
Darien, CT

Emotional Intelligence allows us to better direct our thoughts, feelings and desires so that we are not prisoners of their power. In this way we can build greater access to our emotions and curtail negative thinking for more balance, which helps our brains develop new neurons that make our minds sharper with faster thinking, improved memory and language skills and clearer decision-making while slowing the normal aging process.

Studies indicate that people with developed Emotional Intelligence have a better appreciation of themselves, their values and beliefs, and their boundaries; furthermore they are more inclined to being flexible, optimistic, better communicators, adaptive and build climates of trust and healthy risk-taking, and in addition are better equipped to understand and appreciate others. Also Emotional Intelligence is a good predictor of success –including financial success.

The best news, however is that Emotional Intelligence promotes sharper minds as it ensures that the growth of new brain cells are for positive purposes. Having a sharp mind dramatically increases the probability of staying mentally and physically fit throughout our lives, which translates directly into improved quality of our lives and providing more fulfilling experiences and the direct benefits of better short and long-term memory, ease of decision-making, clarity of vision, increased empathy and improved life quality.

Memory tends to fade for people over 60 years old. What about Emotional Intelligence? Does that fade with age?

San Diego, CA

Our memories and indeed our brains and emotional intelligence will fade if we do not use and challenge them. Age actually is not the key factor except that as we get older and more experienced we tend to lessen the challenges we put to our minds and bodies. Emotional Intelligence helps us ensure that the brain's cellular growth is put to positive use and ensures sharp minds; we can do this by focusing on new challenges, giving it novel situations that take us out of our comfort zone, which will set off the process leading to Brain Fitness.

Developing Emotional Intelligence helps us ensure that this new brain cell growth is positive and to our advantage and thus negates the impact of negative thinking and strong emotions that keep us chained into loop thinking and weighs us down so that we feel stuck. With Emotional Intelligence we re-establish balance and our free will and thereby promote advantageous brain cell growth that helps our memory, speed and thoroughness of thinking and a greater range of feelings for ourselves and others.

As demonstrated by research in order to retain and improve our memories and our Emotional Intelligence-- we will "lose it if we do not use it".

Is there a direct correlation between Emotional Intelligence and IQ? In other words, do people with high IQs tend to have high Emotional Intelligence?

San Diego, CA

Not necessarily. Sheldon in the TV show "Big Bang Theory" is a theoretical physicist whose IQ is so high that he would have to lose 60 points to be considered "smart", yet he possesses a much undeveloped Emotional Intelligence that lacks empathy, cannot detect emotions expressed by others, is incapable of modulating his relationship strategies and cannot identify detect sarcasm or irony.

IQ does tend to remain stable throughout our lives but we can learn Emotional Intelligence and develop it throughout our lives. People with high IQs may well be exposed to more data about Emotional Intelligence and therefore could be motivated to learn more and develop their own Emotional Intelligence. So some spurious correlation may exist but this does not necessarily mean there is a direct correlation between the two. Data on IQ and EQ shows that success —as measured by dollar earnings and promotions – is twice as likely with developed EQ than IQ; moreover people with high Emotional Intelligence were rated as being likeable and good role models.

The term Emotional Intelligence was first brought to a wide audience by Daniel Goleman-with his 1995 book of the same name - in which, and in later works, he argues it takes more than IQ and technical knowledge to be successful at work; indeed he demonstrated the value of Emotional Intelligence for success, corporate productivity, customer satisfaction and effective leadership and communication.

So, while no statistical link is evident, nonetheless it behooves everyone—including those with high IQs to examine and, where appropriate, revise their Emotional Intelligence levels.

Is there a pill that will boost all the good habits of high Emotional Intelligence?

San Diego, CA

That would be very convenient!

Some stores may purport to sell such a pill but this is a superb example of *Caveat Emptor* or "buyer beware".

The alternative is that we do it ourselves, which has many advantages; we know what we are getting, it is enjoyable, and is something that demands our participation to give us a very real reward for a job well done.

The relationship I have with my spouse is fine-- so I do not see why I should bother learning more about the four Relationship Strategies, or, indeed about Emotional Intelligence?

Palm Beach Gardens, FL

Many people connect the word relationship with their rapport with their spouse or significant other and think that the word is limited to than connotation. This actually is how it is interpreted in many magazines but that is totally inaccurate. We have relationships with everyone with whom we have a connection in our lives—including ourselves, everyone we work or socialize with, or relate to.

Relationship, contrary to common parlance, is not limited to that special one. We have multiples of relationships and how we react within each depends on our choice of one of the four strategies we can deploy. With Emotional Intelligence we can become aware of what our default strategy when under stress, and when to use each of the four possibilities to best effect.

Moreover, we develop in relationships. They impact our actions and reactions and influence our whole emotional and thinking processes and our emotional competences and the learning that continues over our lifetimes. So relationships help us develop our Emotional Intelligence and vice versa as Emotional Intelligence does not exist apart from relationships.

The key in Emotional Intelligence is to have flexibility to select the appropriate strategy. At times it is desirable to function in an interdependent manner, which is highly collaborative; at other times, it is most effective to move to independence, where one works alone, and take direct authority of others; or at other times it is more useful to cede that authority and take order as loyal, dependent person; finally there may be times when it is more appropriate to leave the relationship entirely—either just emotionally or both physically and emotionally.

All strategies have value and all are appropriate depending on the context and the relationship. One strategy may work well for some situations but we all need the adaptability and flexibility to modify that strategy with our special other and with all our other relationships in our lives.

What kind of Problems will I experience if I do not develop my Emotional Intelligence?
Palm Beach Gardens, Fl

Contrary to tone of this question, its construction actually requires a certain level of well developed Emotional Intelligence!

A person with poorly developed Emotional Intelligence will most likely have difficulty in relationships:- often finding them unsatisfying or might easily disconnect from others or stay too long in unhealthy relationships, and may find healing from relationship hurt is slow and takes a very long time. This person will tend to be highly reactive, and have a low capacity for chaos, tend to be rigid or brittle under stress, and can become immobilized, moody, resistant, or erratic under duress. This person is likely to have low trust in self and others, and may even discount advice given by others or may not listen to one's own inner voice.

Such a person is likely to have a narrow range of emotions to rely on for information input as internal barriers may prevent that flow; this person will have little emotional empathy for self or for another—either in accurately assessing the empathy level of someone else or in offering compassion. Unsurprisingly this person will lack a balanced reliance on thoughts, feelings, wants, and will be prone to acting on impulse without adequate emotional control.

Fortunately we all can choose to expand our Emotional Intelligence development.

Do we really need emotions to live?

Jupiter, FL

As human beings we experience feelings and emotions; this is an inescapable fact. These emotions are stored in the amygdala as memories of every emotion we have ever felt. The amygdala sends impulses to another part of the brain to activate other regions that set off reflexes—including facial expressions and the activation of several chemical that are associated with emotions.

On the other hand our thoughts stem from our Neocortex shared by mammals –including animals; yet in humans it is responsible for higher functions that endow thoughts with sensory perception, spatial reasoning, conscious thought and language. This is the "gray matter" referred to by Hercules Poirot in solving mysteries.

It contains 100 billion cells, each with 1,000 to 10,000 connections, and has roughly 100 million meters of wiring, all packed into a structure the size and thickness of a formal dinner napkin. The cells in the neocortex are arranged in different regions that permit vision, hearing, a sense of touch and balance, movement, and speech. It is the source of rational and logical thinking and gives us the capacity to think; however that rationality can be off kilter as Byron Katie has demonstrated based on the accuracy of data inputted, which, if incorrect will yield some misperceptions and can lead to problems.

So we have two separate phenomena: - emotions and thoughts; each stored separately and each have their own mechanism for triggering action.

All humans come with both. Sometimes when there has been damage these can be jeopardized. Moreover, we can also attempt to suppress our emotions to avoid feelings that might cause us anxiety; yet as our emotions are an integral part of us they will re-emerge at some point.

Emotions serve a vital function to provide provides us with valuable information as we interact with others and in different life situations; our feelings inform us about the importance of something or someone and gives our experience meaning. The core emotions are anger, anxiety, fear, joy, love, sadness and shame, and these are the primary drivers of actions and decisions.

Emotions also serve the function of providing a supportive guide to support wise decision-making and permit us to make decisions about the type of relationship strategies to use according to the situation;

whether to use the interdependent, independent, dependent or disconnected strategies.

Each of these strategies have their uses and strong points but we have to modulate their use and our respective levels of trust in ourselves and in the other—a feat we can only do if we have emotions.

Can I trust my emotions especially in financial matters?

Paris, France

Despite the value we often put on our thoughts and reason, our emotions are more powerful than our intellect. "In moments of emergency, our emotional centers actually commandeer the rest of the brain…", Goleman, McKee, and Boyatkis (2002), so when faced with matters of complexity—such as detailed financial matters our emotions tend to override our rational thinking and often we go into the fight or flight mode which may follow an emotional impulse and ignore the data in a given situation; this is unlikely to be effective.

We are made up of our emotions and feelings and they give us a vital dimension to know ourselves better, better understand others. We cannot totally eliminate our emotions, and with Emotional Intelligence we can learn to live with them and profit from them by better understanding ourselves and others; moreover EQ helps access relevant feeling so that we re-establish our balance.

So when faced with panoply of financial data, we can take a step back and request more input so that we are able to make a rational decision, instead of triggering an emotional response that continues to be less effective.

I have read that Love is a Decision and we can decide whether or not to love someone, and this is more changeable while my values do not vary. Is this accurate?

Jupiter, FL

We all have a number of core emotions, and love is one of them. All our experiences throughout our lives related to this emotion are stored in our amygdala, and when this feeling is triggered it sets off a chemical reaction that stimulate the production of dopamine, norepinephrine and epinephrine. Love, therefore is an emotion, and while it is changeable, it is not that easy to do so quickly. Our thoughts are easier to change.

However, if we make a decision it will be based on our underlying emotions that set up our thoughts. To love or not is not premised on rational facts alone, as our thoughts, but the panoply of feelings under that emotional label. Hence, we can decide whether we buy flowers for someone, but not whether we love or not.

This is an area replete with confusion. As mentioned earlier, feelings and thoughts are often misconstrued; often as we use terms like "I feel tired" to connote a thought and not a feeling. The confusion can thrive, as some books are structured on this misunderstanding and deviation from the precise definition used in the behavioral sciences.

For instance, a book called "Love is a Decision" by Gary Smalley and

John Trent, suggest that love is a decision and not a feeling—even though this statement is not supported by any validity or reliability testing. Indeed the authors, Smalley and Trent, affirm that this is so; this is turn means that we should be capable of shutting down part of our brain's (amygdala) reaction to send impulses to the hypothalamus to activate the nervous system and thereby trigger reflexes, changed facial expressions and the production of dopamine, norepinephrine and epinephrine. Clearly we cannot do this.

It is possible that the authors -Smalley and Trent- may be viewing this emotion as a thought, and correctly suggest that thoughts are more malleable than emotions although the change still requires an active process. The thought --"I feel tired"—can be changed by addressing this logically in a discussion and mentioning how hours sleep a person may have had, or using biofeedback, and if expertly guided while meditating.

An emotion is harder to alter but not only do we retain all emotions we have ever felt, and so some may no longer apply, but we can use various strategies to rein them in and boosting our Emotional Intelligence is an effective way to ensure that we are aware of our emotions and they are "not wagging the dog".

Our values and beliefs are important elements of our conscious and sub-conscious being as they act as prisms that filter the information we receive and impact how we feel and consequently our thoughts that are molded by our feelings. In their book, authors, Smalley and Trent link their proposal to Christian values of honor, perception of value and worth in another, and advocate being tender and kind. Furthermore, they opine that Love is a reflection of how much we honor another and see their worth and their value, and cite Mathew

6:21 "where your treasure is, there your heart will be also", also in Proverbs 15:1., that tenderness, in the emotion of love, is "a soft answer turns away anger". This is highly laudable and an eminent model to follow for all adherents of all religions.

Yet do these values change? Our values are very important to us and form an integral part of identity, and as such have a major impact on our emotions. Values are important components of our emotions or feelings and while they do not mutate spontaneously they still are capable of being modified over time or with a major catalyst. There are numerous examples of people who have adapted another religion and have absorbed most the base-line values of that religion over time.

Values, like our emotions, can be altered over time and with conscious effort. Developing our Emotional Intelligence improves our ability to get more in touch with our emotions and the underlying values and beliefs. EI gives us additional tools to differentiate between thoughts and our emotions and understand ourselves and others better.

So although we cannot decide whether we love or not we can be true to our values and feelings so that we live with integrity and are able to reclaim our soul and know ourselves.

I have a client who is distanced from her emotions.
Married with children, she is a doctor and is unable
to connect on an intimate level with anyone. Are there
strategies to help reclaim an emotional life and increase
our EQ?

Denver, CO

Our emotions are vital and are an integral part of who we are. They determine how we react to our environment and with other people and their environments. It is not uncommon for some people not to be in touch with their emotions; this is sometimes a result of how we were raised and the environment we encountered as very young children. The emotions are there but suppressed and the individual focuses on thoughts and rational action which can be effective in getting things done, but less effective for that individual to be aware of themselves and further develop Emotional Intelligence and nurture positive brain growth and a sharper mind.

I have outlined a number of strategies but one relatively quick one I have used successfully with clients is to get the client to differentiate between thoughts and feelings. It becomes easy to see the link, and that feelings generally produce thoughts, which in turn produce body sensations and then actions with consequences which produce feelings etc.. This is particularly helpful where the client is smart and action-oriented; by encouraging the individual to take a step back from the action and its propelling reason to identify the prior feelings that actually produced the thought and set the whole chain going.

An example of emotions would be "I feel anxious"; while, an example, of related thinking would be that "I think you are driving too fast". The consequent example of a body sensation might be "I feel stomach pain'; and the action example might be to grab onto the dashboard. This set of events can then set off a feeling of "being fearful"; a thought that "you don't know how to drive" and an action of shouting at the driver.

As indicated above the all highly linked and emotions lead to thoughts and ultimately actions which spur more feelings. The following chart can help a person write about something troubling that elicited emotions, feelings and actions.

❖ Think of a recent troubling issue in your life and describe how you react.

_____

❖ What event or situation started you on the chain to your behavior?

_____

❖ Complete the following; proceed across each line & start from left.

My Feelings	My Thoughts	My Body	My action	What happened
My Feelings	My Thoughts	My Body	My action	What happened
My Feelings	My Thoughts	My Body	My action	What happened
My Feelings	My Thoughts	My Body	My action	What happened
				Etc.

Image 19:- Worksheet

After filling out a worksheet the client goes back and indicates where things could have been changed, which is often at the thinking level or possibly at the feeling level; then one can see how we can gain mastery over our thinking and/ or emotions so that we can alter our behaviors, their consequences and subsequent thoughts and feelings.

Does multitasking improve with Emotional Intelligence?

Palm Beach, FL

Multitasking is a skill that we now require in the 21 st century as information and tasks proliferate. We often have no choice as the speed and complexity of our lives have expanded exponentially. We all have to multi-task —at least to some extent; some people do it badly and cannot focus on any one of the multiple tasks on their plate and seem to get lost in space, while other excel. The prime difference is the level of Emotional Intelligence we bring to this activity.

Despite the preponderance of academic arguments that categorically deny that we are able to both multitask and perform well—especially psychologist, Mihaly Csikszentmihalyi, who argues against multitasking in his book "Flow". To Csikszentmihalyi we need to be fully absorbed in one situation at a time as it takes our focus and attention. Certainly there is much merit to this view. Yet these days necessity is "the mother of invention" and multitasking is practically a requirement these days.

Consequently new skills have developed that require a good basis in developed Emotional Intelligence as:-

- Good multi-taskers have acquired speed to focus on each situation quickly, adapt themselves to any changes, and make decisions quickly.
- Efficiency at multitasking requires flexibility to balance several ideas in the head at the same time, and move easily from one to another.

- Problem-solving is a prime component of multitasking as the person needs to be able to dissect complex arguments to their essential components quickly and effectively.
- It stimulates our memory as multi-taskers must keep track of several key ideas at the same time, and exemplifies the "use it or lose it" mantra.
- Finally good multi-taskers will be able to maintain focus on several items and extract their important elements while avoiding distractions.

To be successful at multitasking we need EI- to manage our lives, overcome hurdles, and to direct our moods and thinking.

Are there specific ways that improve Emotional Intelligence?

San Diego, CA

Improving Emotional Intelligence varies for each one of us and according to our circumstances. We do not have to excel at all facets but we do need to reach at least a "fit" or "very fit" level. Here is a summary of the ten ways described in the book to boost your Emotional Intelligence:-

1. Label your feelings:--not people or situations.	Examples "I <u>feel</u> impatient" instead of "This is ridiculous." "I <u>feel</u> hurt and bitter" instead of "You are an insensitive jerk."

2. Distinguish between thoughts and feelings.	We often use the "feel" word to describe a thought. Example "I feel as if I am talking to a wall"--this is a thought that I think I am not being heard.
3. Take more responsibility for your feelings.	Identify feelings and claim them as yours. This distinguishes you from feeling a victim to the actions of others. E.g. "I feel jealous." vs. "You are making me jealous."
4. Use your feelings to help you and others make decisions.	E.g. "How will I feel if I do this?" "How will I feel if I don't"
5. Show respect for other people's feelings.	Example: Ask "How will you feel if I do this?"
6. Focus on the positive, isolate each feeling, and feel energized, not angry.	Example: Instead of feeling overwhelmed by negative emotions, isolate each one, and tackle each one separately --feel energized and take positive and productive action
7. Validate other people's feelings	Show empathy, understanding, and acceptance of other people's feelings.

8. Practice getting a positive value from your emotions.	Ask yourself how you would feel without the negative emotion and what would help you feel better? E.g. Ask -- "What would help you feel better?"
9. Listen; don't advise, control, criticize, judge.	Instead, try to just listen with empathy and non-judgment.
10. Avoid people who invalidate or constantly criticize you.	While this is not always possible, at least spend less time with them, and focus on your strengths rather than letting them diminish you.

Image 20:- Tips to Boost EQ

Can we build a reserve capacity for sharper minds?

New York City, NY

Studies indicate that we can build up a reserve capacity that can help us with faster and more accurate data processing, better memories and improved overall functioning even when we have not been actively pursuing activities that boost our positive brain cell growth. This is like a reserve tank that keeps us going for a while.

Work by Dr. David Bennett at Rush University in Chicago, does show that we can build surplus reserve capacities by stimulating activities over and above those needed for current requirements; moreover this work goes on to show that the mental reserve capacity can modulate brain damage by warding off the development of

Alzheimer's disease. So far this is the only data on developing sharp minds and Alzheimer's, but it is promising.

It is possible that this reserve capacity operates like a mental savings account that we can draw on when needed, and it argues in favor of continuously building our Brain Fitness, not only for the current benefits, but also as a form of insurance against future dangers of mental decline.

Does having a positive Emotional Intelligence and a sharp mind prevent disease?

San Diego, CA

We have a lot of evidence that attaining and maintaining a sharp mind- with improved Emotional Intelligence- will boost our quality of life and improve our cognitive functions; this helps make faster decisions, improve our focus and heighten our empathy and self-awareness.

Clearly these attributes will help stave off many potential illnesses and help us recuperate from problems faster. Even medical science rarely uses the term of "preventing" an illness as science is barely there yet. However, there is evidence to indicate that positive Emotional Intelligence and sharper minds do extend our mental capacities so that we boost the quality of our lives.

Additionally, one study of patients with Alzheimer's diagnosis (by Dr. Bennett- cited in my earlier book), undergoing Brain Fitness and Emotional Intelligence exercises showed that a good proportion of his sample patients did not develop the full symptoms with the tangles and plaques of Alzheimer's. The explanation suggested by the study was that these people had sufficient reserve capacity of sharper minds to exhibit good thinking skills and showed no clinical signs of the Alzheimer's illness.

So this is an area that requires further research but indications so far are mostly positive.

Do we get more Emotionally Intelligent with experience?
Jupiter, FL

Yes, in principle, we do develop more Emotional Intelligence with experience –if we so choose. It does not come automatically, but Emotional Intelligence is dynamic and can develop throughout our lives as we acquire more experience.

Getting older is unavoidable but falling apart is not and as mentioned previously we "lose it if we do not use it". So if we choose to develop our Emotional Intelligence we can acquire better over our thinking and our emotions, expand our empathy and improve our relationships.

Inertia can strike and perversely we run the greatest danger of inadequately challenging our minds as we gather more experience, and become less energetic about our continuing educational and learning goals. We may be more tempted to stick with patterns or activities we prefer or know, and cruise along in comfort while perhaps our minds wander to other matters. It is when we think that something can be handled easily without undue attention and effort that run the risk of letting our minds slip. Memory also can be an area that we often take for granted and it too responds well to being used frequently.

Consequently challenges such as learning new languages, socializing and learning new things and names, as well as using our palette of emotions and our thinking minds all help trigger reactions in the brain circuitry and get us out our comfort zones so that we stay alert, notice more, and keep our emotional intelligence flourishing.

Do memory exercises—such as crosswords —improve our Emotional Intelligence?

San Diego, CA

Memory exercises are part of the ways to boost the creation of new brain cells that contribute to Brain Fitness and all the related benefits –such as improved short and long- term memory, decision-making, ease of assessing and making judgments, greater empathy. These do contribute to boosting our emotional intelligence, and the inverse is also true that boosting our emotional intelligence contributes to our abilities to ensure positive brain growth and consequent sharpening of our Minds.

Given the malleability of our brains, if we pursue mental exercises –such as crossword puzzles, but more importantly we need to pursue challenging physical aerobic activities, (as these account for about 60% of potential brain cell growth) we will be able to set in motion the processes to generate new brain cells, and boosting emotional intelligence helps us to take back more control over our memory, our emotions, our thought processes and executive abilities and also boost our empathy and personal satisfaction. In other words we will add an improved qualitative dimension to our lives.

Do women and Men have different levels of Emotional Intelligence?

Jupiter, FL

The focus of Emotional Intelligence is not on gender but there are varying levels of development according to each person, and the focus of a consultant is to help each client build in areas that have been identified with the client for more development.

Emotional Intelligence begins as a child who acquires skills, builds competencies to gain accurate self-assessment or communication skills to clearly articulate a thought or deal with conflict, and be able to choose a relationship strategy and develop empathy. These are the building blocks for all Emotional Intelligence.

Brain Quiz No. 8

A blind beggar had a brother who died.

*What relation was the blind beggar
to the brother who died?*

Conclusion

Developing Emotional Intelligence helps us ensure that this new brain cell growth is positive and to our advantage and thus negates the impact of negative thinking and strong emotions that keep us chained into loop thinking and weighs us down so that we feel stuck; moreover inhibits Brain Fitness. This book complements my previous book on "Brain Fitness; Breakthrough Training for those Who Mind" that promotes the feasibility and utility of Brain Fitness by promoting the need for Emotional Intelligence Fitness.

With this combination we dramatically increase the probability of staying mentally and physically fit throughout our lives, it improves our memory, empathy, self-knowledge, awareness of another, clarity of vision, gives us better communication and leadership skills and improved relationships with an informed choice of relationship strategies.

Image 21:- Jupiter Beach, FL

This book empowers the reader to finesse Brain Fitness and all its benefits and advances the developments of Emotional Intelligence to promote self-awareness and control over emotions, which are an integral part of who we are. This allows us greater self-knowledge of our feelings, thoughts and reactions so that we are not their prisoners but are empowered to live our lives in accordance with our values.

Answers to Brain Quizzes

Chapter One

Billy has 39
Bobby has 29
Buzz has 35
Brenda 20

Total = 123

Chapter Two

The numbers are organized by shape.
Look at Row A — they are all rounded shapes.
Row C is all linear shapes.
And Row B is a mix of curves and lines.
Therefore, 16 goes to B, 14 goes to C, and 38 goes to A.

Chapter Three

How many F's did you count?

The answer is six! :

FINISHED FILES ARE THE
RESULT OF YEARS OF SCIENTIFIC
STUDY COMBINED WITH THE
EXPERIENCE OF YEARS

Chapter Four

A study revealed that, in spite of the fact that the puppies are identical; a person under stress would find differences between the two puppies. The more differences a person finds between the puppies, the more stress that person is experiencing.

Chapter Five

Bulb puzzle solution

- Keep the first switch on for a few minutes
- It get warm
- So you switch it off and switch on another one
- Walk into the room with the bulbs, touch them to feel for the warm one, and the others will be on or cold.

Chapter Six

1. (7x4)-8 = 20
2. (3x9)-7 = 20
3. (3x8)-4 = 20
4. The answer is 3.

Chapter Seven

Use two cuts to cut the cake into four equal pieces.

Use your third cut to cut the four pieces in half horizontally (perpendicular to the first two cuts).

Chapter Eight

The blind beggar was the *sister* of her brother, who died.

Bibliography

Bar-On Reuven and Parker, J., (ed.) (2000). *The Handbook of Emotional Intelligence.* Jossey-Bass; San Francisco, CA.

Begley, Sharon, (2007). *Train your Mind, Change your Brain.* Ballantine Books. New York, NY.

Boyatkis, Richard & McKee, Annie (2005). "Resonant Leadership". Harvard Business School Press, Boston, MA.

Csikszentmihalyi, M. (1990). *Flow.* Harper Perennial; New York, NY.

Goleman, D. (1995). *Emotional Intelligence.* Random House ; New York, NY.

Goleman, D. (2000).*Working with Emotional Intelligence.* Bantam Books; New York, NY.

Goleman, D. (2006). *Social Intelligence.* Bantam Books; New York, NY.

Goleman, D., Boyatkis, R. & McKee, A. (2002). *Primal Leadership.* Harvard Business School Press; Boston, MA.

Katie, B. Retrieved form the website www.TheWork.com; June 1, 2012.

Kuehn, B "Strategies for staying sharp" JAMA 2006 Vol. 295 No. 5, February 1, 2006

Legato, Marianne Legato & Tucker, Laura (2005) "Why men never remember and why women never forget". Holtzbrinck publishers: New York, NY.

Linehan, M. (1993). *Cognitive-Behavioral Treatment of Borderline Personality Disorder* . The Guilford Press; New York, NY.

Nadler, R. (2007). *Leaders' Playbook*. Psyccess Press; Santa Barbara, CA.

Ochsner, Kevin. (2008). "The Science of Managing Fears". Neuroscience conference in New York on October 29, 2008.

Polya, A. J. (2009). *Brain Fitness: Breakthrough Training for those Who Mind*. Xlibris; USA.

Prime, P. Retrieved from the website: - www.E21C.org; 1 June 2012.

Lewis, T., Amini, F. & Lannon, R. (2000). *A General Theory of Love*. Random House; New York, NY.

Short, R. R. (1998). *Learning in Relationship*. Foundation for Personal and Professional Success; USA.

Siegel, Daniel. *(1999).The Developing Mind: How Relationships and the Brain Interact to Shape Who We Are.* The Guilford Press; New York, NY.

Smalley, G. & Trent, J.. (1993). *Love is a Decision.* Pocket Books; New York, NY.

Images (-including Tables)

Edwards Brothers Malloy
Thorofare, NJ USA
September 6, 2012